WHITEHEAD WORD BOOK:
A Glossary with Alphabetical Index to Technical Terms in *Process and Reality*

D1319267

by
John B. Cobb, Jr.

P&F Press is the publishing division of Process & Faith, a program of the Center for Process Studies and Claremont School of Theology.

Visit **P&F** Press at

WWW.PROCESSANDFAITH.ORG

ISBN 978-0-9742459-6-6
Printed in the United States of America

CONTENTS

THE INDEX

INTRODUCTION

GUIDE TO THE USE OF THE GLOSSARY

To find where a term is treated in the text, turn to the index on pages xx-xx. If the word is in one or more titles of sections in the glossary, the page number in the glossary will give the page number where the section begins.

When you turn to the text, the term you seek will appear in bold print or in the title of a section. If it is in the title of the section, it will be highlighted in bold only in its first use. If it is elsewhere, it will be highlighted once in each paragraph where it appears. The terms "actual entity" and "actual occasion" appear so frequently throughout the glossary that we have decided not to highlight them except in their first appearance in the glossary as a whole.

PREFATORY COMMENTS

This glossary is intended as a companion to the study of *Process and Reality*. *Process and Reality* is a difficult book, but many of us think it is a profound and profoundly revelatory one. It teaches us to see the world in a new way. And some of us find that this new way illuminates much that has been otherwise obscure. *Process and Reality* brings together much that has been fragmented in the modern world. In short, it is eminently worth studying.

Can it be made more accessible? Certainly it is possible to express ideas that the new way of seeing supports in quite simple and easily understood language. Years ago Donald Sherburne produced an abridged version of

Process and Reality that made it more available to students. He included a short glossary. C. Robert Mesle has written an introduction to Whitehead that makes much of his thinking remarkably accessible. (See *Process-Relational Philosophy: An Introduction to Alfred North Whitehead.* Templeton Foundation Press, 2008.) Also, there is much writing in theology and some other fields that has developed the application of elements of Whitehead's thought in quite simple terms. Mesle himself is the author of the most readable introduction (*Process Theology,* Chalice Press, 1993). Of course, part of the richness and precision of Whitehead's thought is lost in these simplifications. Nevertheless, much is also communicated. Much more of this kind of writing is still needed.

But if one wants to grapple with Whitehead's thinking for oneself, one still needs to read his own formulations. There is finally no substitute for the study of *Process and Reality.* Since one of the obstacles to reading this book is the large number of technical terms, a glossary can help. It has been suggested that there is need of a much more extensive glossary than Sherburne provided, one with fuller explanations of Whitehead's many technical terms. The present work is an attempt to respond to that suggestion.

In developing this glossary, I have tried to be as faithful as I can to Whitehead's intentions as he wrote *Process and Reality.* However, the same warning that is needed with respect to secondary literature generally, applies here as well. Every explanation of a text is also an interpretation limited to the understanding of the interpreter and influenced by the views of the interpreter. I have tried to check against personal idiosyncrasies in interpretation by inviting other Whitehead scholars to criticize what I have done. I have reasonable confidence that what I have written, with their help, is reasonably accurate.

Readers can be helped to understand the text by this kind of glossary, but in the long run, as they study the text they may, indeed they should, come to their own interpretation. Even if one does not judge that I have made egregious errors, there are, unquestionably, nuances that I have neglected or missed altogether that may prove important—even perhaps more important than the meanings I have rightly discerned. Sometimes fresh insight into a single term can have extensive ramifications.

Furthermore, it would be foolish to suppose that every technical term employed by Whitehead has exactly the same meaning in each use. Whitehead was thinking while he wrote. New insights came to him. He did not always re-write what he had written before in light of these insights. Often these are additions to, rather than corrections of, what he had previously written, but even additions change the context of everything. Meanings cannot be static in a changing context. Lewis Ford has gone to great lengths to analyze Whitehead's thought at various stages as he wrote this book. Some of his judgments are disputable, but the overall point that Whitehead worked through several stages of understanding during the writing is not.

Finally, Whitehead would be the last person to think of his book as a final statement. It invites continuing reflection and revision. My personal judgment is that none of its would-be revisers thus far have even caught up with Whitehead's insights, much less surpassed them in any general way. When making this statement I especially refer to revisions I have myself proposed. I and others may be right on specific points, but none of us have come close to encompassing his work in a larger, more illuminating context.

This does not mean that efforts to go beyond his accomplishments should cease. One reason for trying to make understanding of Whitehead's text easier is that this may make it possible for students more quickly to grasp accurately what he proposes and then genuinely go beyond him, for example, in his physics. Most of the efforts of my generation were exhausted by the struggle to understand. Most of our proposals for going beyond are based on an inadequate grasp of what Whitehead had himself accomplished.

It is important to realize in a deeper way the limits of what a glossary can do. Those who want help in understanding Whitehead sometimes suppose that the problem is simply that he chose to express himself in a difficult technical language. They think that all that is necessary is to translate this language into one they already understand.

This is a serious error. No deeply original thinking can be expressed adequately in existing language. That language operates among people who see the world in a particular way. The deeply original thought leads to a different way of seeing the world. It has to work against the implications of the existing language. It has to draw the readers or the hearers into noticing features of experience that have heretofore eluded them. It has to evoke to consciousness dim intuitions that have been suppressed by the existing conceptuality and socialization. One cannot translate the new vision into the vocabulary of the old. In Jesus' words, this would be to pour new wine into old wineskins.

This is why Whitehead is so alien to the dominant form of philosophy in the English-language world. This philosophy takes ordinary language as its object. It undertakes to clarify that language but to use nothing else. In other words, it assumes that meaningful communication can occur only in ordinary language. Whitehead, on the other hand, believed that reality is quite different from the way it was understood during the period that ordinary English developed. There is much wisdom embodied in that language, but there is truth that cannot be directly expressed in it.

What *is* possible? More that two millennia ago, Buddhists faced a similar problem. They had come to insights that those of Whitehead today remarkably resemble. They found that their insights showed that the conceptuality that informed their language was inherently misleading. It reified what is in fact fluid. It gave the impression that things exist in themselves in separation from others when in fact they exist only in their relationships. They judged that their new insights were of the greatest psychological and spiritual value. Yet they decided that these insights could not be expressed in language. Hence they developed techniques of meditation that broke the power of linguistic and conceptual thought and opened one to what happens as it happens.

Obviously, Whitehead did not follow that procedure. In the Western tradition philosophers had frequently expressed new insights partly in existing language and partly by creating new terms. The new terms appeal for new insights on the part of readers, but the philosopher discusses them extensively in more familiar language in order to aid in the attainment of the new insight. Whitehead continued that tradition.

It may be, however, that the novelty of his vision is greater than that of his predecessors or, at least, is more sharply at odds with the inherited language. His task is to use one language to point to insights that are quite different from those that language normally conveys. He introduces new terms and concepts to give expression to these insights, in some sense, to fix them. Clearly a glossary cannot simply translate all these terms back into ordinary language.

But if that is not possible, what is? The simple alternative is to define each term in the glossary in its relation to the other terms there. That is, of course, useful and even necessary for a grasp of the system. But one could then learn the system without really gaining the insights that make it significant. I have little interest in advancing this kind of study of Whitehead. Whitehead's thought developed as a penetration into what is, grounded in

the growing conviction that what truly *is* is experience. The whole conceptuality must have its exemplification in experience and in the interpretation
of things in terms of that experience. If the concepts are learned in terms
of verbal definitions without this experiential content and basis, the study
of his philosophy becomes just a game. Coming to new ways of seeing the
world, however, is not a game. It is existential transformation—as Buddhists saw long ago and as the Greeks also understood.

Struggling with these problems can make one sympathetic with the Bud-
dhist solution. The reifications and the substantialist implications pervading
the old language do not disappear in the new. Without constant recourse to
the basic intuitions, the new conceptuality fails to make the break. This was
part of Whitehead's own struggle. His intuitions often outran his concepts,
and his concepts only went part of the way to express them. Concepts
do seem inherently reifying as Buddhists suppose, and Whitehead's own
concepts are not free of this tendency. Without meditation of some sort,
one cannot enter into the Buddhist/Whiteheadian vision.

I believe that a distinctively Whiteheadian meditation has its place.
This meditation goes back and forth between the verbal expression of
intuitions and the examination of experience to test their value. This
meditation should not end when one concludes that one has an understanding of what Whitehead is saying, but that by itself is an important
step. Whitehead's proposals call for continuous testing against experience
and unending further development. But for the present, just getting to a
basic understanding is the goal.

The scope of experience in relation to which **intuitions** are tested is far
wider in Whitehead than it has been thus far in Buddhism. Whitehead
thought that results of empirical study of the world must also be taken
into account. Some of his intuitions arose in his attempt to understand
the empirical data of the physics of his day rather than in direct phenomenological inspection. Some of his intuitions were about how to bring
these two fields of thought together. One reason that Whitehead could not
agree to the abandonment of conceptual thinking was that science cannot
do without it. At the same time he judged that its further progress was
handicapped by the power of inadequate, inherited concepts. Wherever
intuitions arose, for Whitehead, they must be tested in the sciences as well
as in phenomenological examination of one's own experience.

This understanding of the situation is the context in which I have
struggled with the question, what kind of glossary might prove genuinely

helpful. My answer is, one that helps readers relate Whitehead's technical terms to their experience. Most important here is their immediate personal experience, but their experience also includes their reflection about other philosophers and the current scientific situation. Obviously, especially in these areas, experience varies greatly, and I assume rather little.

The standard way to arrange a dictionary or a glossary is alphabetical. I decided against this. There are too many problems. For example, there are many types of feelings. Should each appear in the glossary alphabetically, or should they all be grouped under feeling? Should they be organized alphabetically as subheadings under feeling or ordered in a more rational way?

In the end, I decided to try to find an organization of terms that developed them in a more rational fashion. I begin with the most basic terms and explain subsequent terms in relation to them. In general, in the discussion of each term, I make minimal use of terms not yet explained. If, for example, a reader looks up "symbolic reference" and finds in the account other unfamiliar terms that are not explained in that section, these terms should be found in the preceding sections.

This structure means that the book requires a separate alphabetical list of terms with indication of where they are chiefly discussed. Readers of Whitehead who find a technical term with which they want help can go directly to this alphabetical list of terms and then to the pages on which they are treated. With this extra step, the book can function as a dictionary.

In the past it has been generally recognized that very few can fruitfully study *Process and Reality* on their own. Coming to an understanding of this book has been a collective task of students over two generations. One needs to study it first with a guide who has benefited from this collective work. This limitation does not apply to any of Whitehead's other writings; so it in no way precludes independent study of his thought.

Reading others of his books, such as *Science and the Modern World* and *Adventures of Ideas*, is to be highly recommended. But I have personally discouraged people, including philosophers, from reading *Process and Reality* by themselves.

It may be, however, that with the use of this guide to Whitehead's technical vocabulary, some students can get sufficient benefit from the collective work of interpretation that has gone on over two generations to read *Process and Reality* on their own. That is an ambitious claim, but I hope it may be tested. Since there are now few places in the United States where seminars on Whitehead's book are offered, it becomes increasingly important that there be other ways of getting access to his most mature and sustained analyses.

The glossary may have a second use. Because the terms are introduced and explained in a rational sequence instead of an alphabetical one, this work can be read through from beginning to end as one more attempt at an introduction to *Process and Reality*. This is not likely to work well for someone who has not previously studied Whitehead. It is not intended as an introduction for the lay reader. For that, I strongly recommend the little book by Mesle. But one who has read Mesle's book might find this a useful next step. Someone who is generally familiar with Whitehead's thought, but who needs an orderly account of its basic ideas, may find it helpful. Nevertheless, its basic use should be as a companion to the study of the text.

In preparing this glossary I have sought, and continue to seek, critical comments from other Whitehead scholars. The present version is indebted to Joseph Bracken and Leemon McHenry. We hope that users of the book will share suggestions for correcting and improving future versions.

Jeanyne Slettom prepared the whole publication and added the index, without which the use of the book would be severely limited.

THE GLOSSARY

SPECULATIVE PHILOSOPHY

Whitehead describes his philosophy as **speculative.** Unfortunately, "speculation" has a bad reputation. It many contexts it means the proposal of ideas without adequate justification. Obviously Whitehead does not advocate this. However, he believes that there is a speculative element in all thought and that this should be acknowledged and carefully constrained.

In the early twentieth century philosophers in the English-language world developed synthetic systems of thought that responded to developments in the sciences. Later in the century there was reaction against this speculative effort to achieve a synthesis as too unreliable and idiosyncratic. It was replaced by analytic philosophizing. Analytic philosophy undertakes clarifying analysis but does not propose syntheses of ideas. On the European continent, the great example of a speculative synthesis was the work of G.W.F. Hegel. Those who reacted against Hegel often turned to phenomenology as a form of careful description and analysis of experience without speculation about its relation to anything else.

Whitehead believed that even those who tried hardest to free themselves from any speculative assumptions did not succeed. In any case his interest was in the synthesizing approach. He thought that new discoveries in physics raised questions that the existing language and assumptions of physicists, *a fortiori,* ordinary language, were not able to handle. There was a need for fundamental re-thinking of the assumptions provided by modern philosophy. Such re-thinking required careful analysis of experience and careful use of language, but these alone were not sufficient. It also required developing new hypotheses that could be tested against data in various fields. The new hypotheses are speculations, and without some speculation, science cannot advance. Whitehead wanted to adopt a similar method in philosophy.

To identify one's philosophy as speculative is emphatically to announce that it does not consist of settled conclusions or doctrines that claim certainty. It consists of the best and most fully tested hypotheses one can currently offer. Part of the test is the way they fit together. Their coherence is as important as their adequacy to account for the data in the various fields of human experience and knowledge.

For Whitehead, nothing in science is beyond the possible need of revision. Certainly this is true of philosophy as well. Hence his philosophy is speculative. Of course, in science some hypotheses have been so thoroughly tested that it is not practically important to stress their speculative character. Other theories are vigorously debated with new tests being devised to test them. They are obviously and thoroughly speculative. In philosophy also this distinction applies. Hence, occasionally Whitehead calls special attention to the fact that some hypotheses are less well tested than others. All are speculative to some degree, but some are much more speculative than others in the sense that evidence in their favor is far less conclusive.

FALLACY OF THE PERFECT DICTIONARY

A perfect dictionary would be one in which some set of words was unambiguously defined and all the others were defined in terms of them. We would then have the possibility of communicating univocally, that is, without the possibility of diverse understanding of what we mean. Whitehead's point is that this is impossible, so that pressing for more and more exact meanings of terms reaches its limits. Sometimes we are reduced to appealing to others for an **intuitive** leap. This is true even in ordinary conversation, but Whitehead is very much aware that as he thinks deeply about the nature of reality, he can only use words that encourage his readers to look in the same direction and see something very much like what he sees. He cannot define what he sees in terms of familiar words. If one looks to this glossary for a "perfect dictionary" of the terms used in *Process and Reality*, one will be disappointed. But that in itself is not a failure of the glossary. A great philosopher invites us to see the world in a different way. *Process and Reality* is such an invitation. This glossary tries to help toward that end.

The **fallacy of the perfect dictionary** is closely related to what today is called by its critics "foundationalism." A reliable foundation on which to construct a system requires that the basic terms by unambiguous or fixed. Logical positivism tried hard to develop a perfect dictionary so that a completely reliable system of philosophy could be based on it. Those whose philosophy consists in the clarification or ordinary language tend to think that it is possible to attain exactitude of meaning in this context. Whitehead thinks that is not possible.

FALLACY OF MISPLACED CONCRETENESS

Whitehead believes that abstractions are of utmost importance. He was himself a mathematician, and he reveled in the many ways in which the mathematical treatment of abstractions has led to new discoveries about the world. He is often criticized for giving too much attention, and too large a role, to what is abstract.

But Whitehead is keenly aware of the difference between the abstract and the concrete. And he recognized that abstractions are often credited with functions they cannot have. They are often treated as if they were concrete. Consider, for example, the statement that Buddhism teaches that all things are impermanent. Of course, one may use it as a shorthand formulation of the fact that most teachers who call themselves Buddhists affirm this. However, one may also forget that it is shorthand for something else and begin to think there is such a thing as Buddhism that has its own essence, acts in this or that way, and can accurately be described as having or lacking particular characteristics.

Similarly, when one asks why an object released at a height falls to the ground, someone may answer that it is because of gravity or, even, the law of gravity. Once again, if this is shorthand for the statement that bodies of various sorts attract one another, there is no harm. But if one begins to think that in addition to the entities that attract one another there is something else named gravity or, even, the law of gravity, one is committing the **fallacy of misplaced concreteness.** This can lead to scientific and metaphysical confusion.

As other philosophers have commented, the map is not the landscape.

Whitehead was a mathematician who saw that much mathematics often committed the fallacy of misplaced concreteness. In concrete experience there are no points. Everything we experience has some extension. The idea of a point is an abstraction. He judged it important to develop a definition of a point that showed how it is derived by abstraction from experience.

Some philosophers object to this distinction between the abstract and the concrete, arguing that the notion of concreteness is itself an illusion. Whitehead affirmed that experience as such is fully concrete or actual and can be contrasted with the abstractions from it. Accordingly, he described the world as made up of "actual entities."

CATEGORIES OF EXISTENCE

Part of the philosophical task is to identify what kinds of things "exist." Of course, that depends on what the philosopher means by "exist." For some philosophers, to exist means to be fully actual as a concrete particular. Whitehead reserves that mode of existence for what is "actual." To exist means to have reality of any kind whatever. Anything that can be thought or imagined "exists" as well as any sort of grouping of things. Nevertheless, among all of these modes of existence, being actual has a certain priority.

ACTUAL ENTITY

This term is not intended by Whitehead to refer to things only as interpreted by his own system. Instead it is intended as a way of referring across systems. Every metaphysics in some way distinguishes what is actual from what is merely possible or **potential**. Imagining things to be different does not mean that the actuality has changed.

One may ask what Descartes thought the actual entities to be. The answer would be material **substances** and mental substances. If one inquired about Plato, in some of his dialogues it may be that the "ideas" are the entities that are truly actual. In Hume it seems that the patches of color and patterns of sound are the actual things. In Kant and Hegel, one might argue that *Geist* is the fully actual entity. For Spinoza it may be that the only actual entity is the whole, identified as either Nature or **God.** For the Greek atomists, the atoms were the actual entities. For Leibniz, it was the monads. Whitehead believed that deciding what sorts of entities are truly concrete or actual is a fundamental task for philosophy and one that is quite relevant for physics as well.

Whitehead's judgment was that the actual entities that make up the world are all **"actual occasions."** That means that they are happenings, occurrences, or **events** rather than substantial entities that endure unchanged through time. A momentary human experience is one example of such an occasion. Explaining what is fully actual and how it occurs is a central task for Whitehead's philosophy.

There is one actual entity, Whitehead taught, that is not an occasion. In contrast, it is everlasting, and in some respects it is eternal. This actual entity is "**God.**" Since for Whitehead God is not an exception to the categories but rather their ideal exemplification, there are many similarities between God and actual occasions. Some who follow Whitehead in many respects believe that it is better to think of God as a series of actual occasions. Whitehead preferred to see God in greater contrast to the ever **perishing** occasions of which the **temporal** world is composed. But he did not think this made God either more or less actual than these occasions. Hence, for him, the class of actual entities is composed of God plus all the occasions that make up the world.

ACTUAL OCCASION

Actual occasions are the actual entities of which the world, meaning thereby this cosmos and any other cosmos that may have been, may now be, or may come to be, is composed. This is a sharp challenge to most of the Western tradition and to the "common sense" inculcated in us by our language. When we say, "the dog barks," or "the rug is blue," most of us think of the dog and the rug as actual entities.

Whitehead disagrees. To understand his thought we must shift from giving priority to what most of our nouns, such as "dog" and "rug" designate to the experience of the one who hears the barking of the dog or sees the blueness of the rug. The dog-as-barking and the rug-as-blue are abstractions from the experience of the individual who is hearing or seeing. It is the experience of the individual that is fully actual.

However, once we understand what kind of thing is actual, we can find actuality also in the barking dog and the blue rug. With the barking dog it is easier. Common sense suggests that the dog is not exhausted by an observer's hearing the barking. The dog also has a point of view. At any given moment there is the dog's experience as well as the observer's. The dog's experience, in each moment, is just as much an actual occasion as is the experience of the human observer. If we go further than that, we get into questions of physics and chemistry that are best dealt with in a different context, that of quantum physics.

For Whitehead there are also quantum events. These, too, are actual occasions. Since everything is composed of them, anyone who believes there really is a world must accord them actuality. Whitehead affirms they are events, but he needs to specify that they are occasions, because events come in all sizes. A war is an event. So is a conversation. But a war or a conversation can be analyzed into the smaller events of which it is composed. Whitehead believes that this process of breaking down larger events into the smaller events of which they are composed must somewhere come to an end. He sometimes writes of electronic and protonic occasions in these terms. But more generally we should think of a quantum of energy as where we arrive at that end. Quanta are now the "atoms" in the original sense of not further divisible units.

The two clearest examples of actual occasions are, thus, a momentary experience, whether of a human being or of some other animal, and a quantum of energy. By giving them the same name, Whitehead calls attention to what, with all their differences, they have in common. First, we may point out what they are not. They are not "**matter**" in the Greek or the modern sense. That is, they are not passive recipients of form or action. They act to constitute themselves as what they become. Second, they become what they become out of a given world. What they are is largely a function of what other things are. In the case of the quantum, it is what it is largely because of the quantum field in which it occurs. In the case of a moment of human experience, it is what it is largely because of the character and content of antecedent human experiences and the neuronal events in the brain. But the principle of uncertainty in the case of the quanta and our awareness of an element of choosing indicate that, however much it is limited by the past, an actual occasion does decide exactly what it will become. Also, in both instances, what it becomes informs future actual occasions. An actual occasion is acted on, it acts in its own synthesizing of its data, and it acts in future occasions. The word "actual" is rich in meaning.

The word "occasion" also distinguishes Whitehead's view of what is actual from many others. Most languages lead their users to suppose that an act requires an actor distinguishable from the act. The actor is normally thought of as acting more than once. This implies that the actor's "self" endures through time and expresses itself in a succession of acts. Similarly, what receives influences from the **past** is thought of as something distinct from those influences. The idea of a **substance** that is acted on and acts is hard to eradicate from our thought. But Whitehead calls us to just such an eradication. An occasion is not something substantial being acted on and acting. It comes into being as the act of receiving and of self constitution. In the case of the quantum we cannot get beyond the energy-event to a particle that is being acted on or acting. If there is a "particle," it is constituted by a succession of actual occasions. Physical things like stones or trees are finally made up of actual occasions. They are not the ultimate actors but rather the outcome of many individual actions of actual occasions.

Similarly, an occasion of human experience is not to be understood as a person experiencing. There is no person beneath or behind the experiencing. The act of taking the **past** into account and constituting itself with a view to the **future** *is* the actual occasion. The person is constituted as a long series of such occasions growing out of one another and out of the body.

Are there actual occasions other than quanta of energy and animal experiences? This is, from a Whiteheadian point of view, a factual question, and it is difficult to ascertain how Whitehead thought about it. He clearly speaks of occasions in "**empty space**," but probably these can be subsumed under quanta of energy. He speaks explicitly of electronic occasions, but if it turns out that electrons can be analyzed into smaller quanta, a possibility he foresaw, if pressed, he would probably withdraw that designation. Some of his language about molecules seems to imply that there are molecular occasions. But this may just be lack of precision.

The most interesting question is whether there are cellular occasions. Whitehead first denies this, but then, after developing the notion of **hybrid feelings**, he seems to allow it. Most of his followers believe that the overall implication of Whitehead's thought is that there are unicellular actual occasions.

Whitehead understood that most of the things we talk about are "**societies**" of diverse kinds, that is, groupings of actual occasions. Some of their characteristics are derivable from the character of the occasions of which they are composed, but they are divisible and, therefore, not actual occasions.

Students of Whitehead have debated these matters extensively. Some have thought that at whatever level we find well-integrated individuals, such as electrons, atoms, and molecules, we should posit actual occasions. It seems that scientists can hardly avoid attributing **causal efficacy** to these entities of a sort that is not wholly derived from the quanta of which they are composed. This suggests either that **societies** have more of the characteristics of individual occasions than Whitehead attributed to them or that there are actual occasions at diverse levels.

For Whitehead these are empirical questions. Actual occasions are the only efficient causes. If in the end the **causality** attributed to an atom can be explained exhaustively in terms of the causality of the quanta of which it is composed, then the atom can be understood as a well integrated **society** of quanta. If not, then either it must be judged that a unique kind of societal causality, not described by Whitehead, emerges at different levels, or that new types of actual occasions emerge at these levels.

OCCASION OF EXPERIENCE

"Occasion of experience" is another name for actual occasion. Hence everything stated above about an actual occasion applies to an occasion of experience. However, the term brings to the fore one of Whitehead's most controversial assertions. There is little problem for most people in agreeing that momentary animal experiences are occasions of experience, but many find it disturbing and implausible to describe quanta of energy in this way. What does it mean, and why does Whitehead take this step?

First, what does it *not* mean? It does not mean that the quanta are **conscious.** The experience attributed to them is nonconscious. It certainly does not mean that they think or have sensory experience. Sensory experience depends on organs of sensation. Thought and consciousness require a brain. All such things are obviously lacking in quanta. If we take the meaning of "experience" from our own and generalize, we must first think only of our preconscious or even nonconscious experience and then of its most general structure. What we would arrive at would be much like what I described above—taking account of the **past,** constituting itself, and affecting the **future.** William James wrote of "throbs of experience." But why use the term "experience?"

One answer is that we have only two sources of concepts. Many concepts are drawn from the objects of our sense experience. Science works chiefly with these. But these concepts all depend on an observer. They characterize what is seen or measured. They tell us nothing about what exists in itself, what is real whether an observer is there or not. The **"objective"** world clearly is not independent of observers. It is what appears to them. It is apparent or phenomenal.

But for Whitehead it was imperative to attribute independent actuality to actual occasions. An **actual world** cannot be composed of appearances alone. The only locus of actuality that we know directly is our own experience, ourselves as **subjects.** The **objective,** the phenomenal, exists only *for* subjects. Only subjects exist for themselves.

Further, only **subjects** are acted on or act. The description given above is, therefore, of a subject. Either the quantum exists in itself or it exists only for observers. Whitehead opts for the view that it exists in itself. There were quantum events long before there were any human beings at all or, indeed, any animal life. Certainly there were quantum events long before humans could, in any sense, observe them.

If quanta are **subjects,** that is, patients and agents that occur whether observed or not, it is not a large leap to call them experiences. Indeed, an experience provides our only clue for conceiving something being acted on and acting. This may seem strange, since notions of **causality** are deeply entrenched in sciences that deal only with phenomena. But David Hume was correct. Among **objective** phenomena there are only **temporal** successions. It is only in experience that we have a clue as to how the **past** informs the present.

To put this in another way, the only notion of **cause** that makes sense is an **internal relation.** The effect is affected but not fully constituted by the cause. In experience, that is a meaningful concept. Apart from experience, it has no meaning at all. Indeed, Whitehead decided that apart from experience there *is* nothing at all. If quanta are actual, they are occasions of experience. This judgment opens the door to further analysis and speculation.

Another way to understand why Whitehead attributes experience to quanta is the assumption that **conscious experience** is the product of evolution. Whitehead thinks it quite understandable that beings with conscious experience have emerged out of beings whose experience is not conscious. We experience in ourselves degrees of consciousness fading off into nonconscious experience. Whitehead is sure that even when we are most acutely conscious a great deal is going on in our experience of which we are not conscious. But it is not meaningful to suppose that experience as such, for example, internalization of the **past** and self constitution, emerges out of **objective** phenomena or out of purely material atoms moving in the void. Evolution requires fundamental continuities underlying the discontinuities. **Subjects** cannot be evolved from a world consisting only of objects. Animal experience cannot emerge out of a complex of neurons understood materialistically or mechanically.

Some Whiteheadians have called Whitehead a "panpsychist," although Whitehead never used that term about his philosophy. Sometimes the term simply means the universal presence of **subjectivity,** in which case it is rightly applied to Whitehead. However, for Whitehead the **"soul"** appears only with the central nervous system, and "soul" is the English translation of "*psyche*." There is a vast difference between the relatively rare occasions of psychic experience and the vastly more numerous occasions of quantum experience. Hence, the term panpsychism is misleading with regard to what Whitehead intends. Some Whiteheadians have proposed "panexperientialism" or "pansubjectivism" as suitable labels. For Whitehead to be actual is to be experiential and to have subjectivity. But he does not use any of these terms to describe his position.

ACTUAL WORLD

The **"actual world"** is the world as actually given for any actual occasion. It is composed entirely of **past** actual occasions or occasions of experience and includes them all. It is, indeed, the past of and for that actual occasion.

Whitehead is influenced by relativity theory in his understanding of the **actual world.** Prior to the emergence of relativity theory it was generally supposed that there is a unique "present" that divides all **events** into the past, the present, and the future. Accordingly, any two events occurring simultaneously would have the same actual world. Whitehead, however, recognized that no two actual occasions can have exactly the same actual world when one understands that the **past** consists of those actual occasions that have **causal efficacy** for the present occasion. The sound of thunder now generated ten miles from me does not become part of my actual world for several seconds. Light now leaving the sun does not become part of the actual world for occasions on earth until it reaches them. If, as Einstein thought, nothing can travel faster than light, then lots of events that I think of as in my past are not part of my actual world.

Whitehead taught that every occasion in my actual world has some effect in my experience now. Obviously, the effect of the vast majority of **past** occasions is negligible, but it is not zero. Everything that happens affects everything that will happen in its future. Indeed, the **future** of an occasion is defined as that which will be causally affected by what the occasion becomes.

EVENTS

Whitehead does not use **"events"** in a technical way. He intends to mean by it what people in general understand by the term. An election is an event; so is a storm; and so also is a conversation. The difference between his understanding of events and the understanding that has dominated so much of Western thought is with respect to the relation of events to the things that make them up. For most modern Westerners an event is explained as what people or animals or other natural actors do and what happens to them. That is, the fully actual entities are thought to be people or things that act or are acted on by other persons or things. The event is thought to have a secondary status. In the thoroughgoing instance of this way of thinking, the event is completely explained as nothing but bits of **matter** in motion.

Whitehead reverses the relation of stable entities and events. The stable entities are ultimately made up of quantum events complexly structured. The events are most concretely analyzed into the smaller events of which they are composed. The events that cannot be analyzed into smaller events, that is, the "atomic" events are the actual occasions or occasions of experience discussed above.

For example, if we take the conversation mentioned above as an example, it can be analyzed into, among other things, the experience of the participants. The experience of each participant can be analyzed into a **temporal** sequence of occasions of experience. One moment of this temporally extended experience is a single occasion of experience. That can be analyzed into its parts, in various ways, but not into complete occasions. In this sense that momentary occasion of experience is atomic.

ETERNAL OBJECTS

After Whitehead has listed **"categories of existence,"** he identifies two of them as having "a certain extreme finality." We have discussed one of these, the actual entities, at some length. The other one is **"eternal objects,"** and we will now turn to them.

To get into the right ball park, we can begin by saying that mathematical forms and formulae are eternal objects and that qualities of all kinds are eternal objects. E=mc squared is an eternal object; so is a definite shade of yellow. These eternal objects are directly illustrated in our world—in quite different ways. Anything that can be abstracted from experience and then can recur is an eternal object. There are also eternal objects that have never been actualized and never will be. A seven-dimensional space, also, is an eternal object, in that it can be thought about by mathematicians.

Most science, both natural and social, deals with eternal objects, although from time to time it must recur to experience, and it intends to make predictions about such experience. For example, based on carefully developed theory one predicts that if conditions of a particular type obtain, an observer of a certain piece of equipment will see a needle point to a definite number. Mathematicians can stay still longer in the realm of the abstract. Every philosophy must find some place for what Whitehead calls eternal objects and give some account of their status.

Whitehead himself gives the following equivalent terms: "**pure potentials for the specific determination of fact**," and "**forms of definiteness**." Occasionally he uses the term "abstract possibility," and students have often made the contrast between eternal objects as pure possibilities and actual entities as possessing full actuality. However, Whitehead generally associates possibility with something that could actually occur. It is better to stay closer to his language. Eternal objects are **pure potentials**, and that means forms that could in principle characterize something actual, but that are in their nature indifferent to whether they do, or ever will, characterize anything actual.

It is well to ask why Whitehead invented the term "eternal object" instead of sticking with the more familiar language of **potentials** and forms. First, **"objects"** establishes their status as depending on **subjects.** Objects exist only for subjects. They can be felt; they cannot feel. In themselves they cannot act. They are, indeed, passive.

We might suppose that all this would be heard in a word like "form," but the history of philosophy warns us that this is not so. The Greeks thought extensively about form and **matter.** They thought everything actual could be understood as formed matter. But in their understanding, "matter" was passive. Acting was a function of form rather than matter. Plato, therefore, attributed an extremely important role to forms.

Further, most of the discussion of forms was of the forms of actual things and norms. Forms were used for classifying, and there was a sense that there were objectively real types of things, just as there were real norms identified by value-laden words. Whitehead wanted a label that would not carry any of these connotations. *Qua* objects, no one form is preferable to any other form. No one classificatory system is better than another. There are hierarchies of forms in terms of complexity, but not in terms of **value.**

Whitehead also wanted to avoid associating his distinction between actual entities and eternal objects with the traditional discussion of particulars and universals. For him every eternal object is a particular, in that it is just what it is and distinct from every other eternal object, but every eternal object is also a universal, in that it is a **potential** for characterizing any actual occasion. Similarly, every actual occasion is both a particular and a universal, since it is just what it is in distinction from every other actual occasion and also a potential for participating in the constitution of any future actual occasion.

Sometimes the eternal objects are explained as abstractions. This, too, can be misleading. It suggests that their initial status is in actual things and that they exist only there or as we abstract from these. Such abstraction certainly occurs, but it has no effect on the character or status of an eternal object. Nevertheless, to say that they are totally abstract may help.

Indeed, it is hard for most people to think at a sufficiently abstract level to understand what eternal objects are and are not. Charles Hartshorne critiqued the idea of eternal objects. One of his objections was that the "existence" of eternal objects undercut the **creativity** and novelty of concrete existence. If everything existed **potentially** before it was actualized, **God** would know all human creations before they were constructed. In that case, Mozart's composition of music and its orchestral renditions would add nothing to God.

From Whitehead's perspective this reflects an insufficiently abstract idea of the eternal objects. It is true that every pattern that is exemplified in every symphony that has ever been written or performed has always existed as an eternal object. Indeed, since no symphony is ever exactly the same in two performances, we must say that there is a slightly different pattern **ingredient** in every performance, and since no two listeners will hear it in exactly the same way, there is a slightly different pattern for every hearer and on each occasion of hearing. But these are only patterns. As patterns they have no different status from trillions of other patterns until they are selected by Mozart and the orchestras that actualize the music.

In any case, as eternal objects they are not patterns of sound. The sound does not exist until it is heard. Even **God** cannot hear it until God can share the hearing with creatures. Similarly, God had no visual experience until there were creaturely eyes.

The choice of the term "eternal" may have been unfortunate. For many people it has a religious, or at least an honorific, connotation. Under the influence of Plato, it was long thought that things that are eternal are somehow superior to things that are **temporal.** But for Whitehead all **value** is located in actuality and all actuality is temporal or, in **God's** case, derivative from what is temporal.

For Whitehead "eternal" means nothing more than nontemporal. That is another way of saying that "eternal" objects have no actuality at all in themselves. They do not come into being and they do not pass away. They are related to every **temporal** moment in the same way, so far as their own nature is concerned.

Some of them do, however, become **ingredient** in actual things. For the analysis of the world this is important. For understanding the eternal objects as such, it makes no difference.

For purposes of thought the typical examples of eternal objects are "**simple.**" A simple eternal object cannot be analyzed any further. A particular shade of yellow is a simple eternal object. Of course, in actual experience we are almost always dealing with "**complex**" eternal objects. When I open my eyes I confront a multiplicity of colors arranged in patterns. The same moment of experience includes sounds, tastes, and tactile feelings as well as emotions, memories, and anticipations. All of these have forms, that is, all are characterized by eternal objects. The eternal object that characterizes my experience as a whole in any moment is very complex indeed.

This distinction is easy to understand, but the idea of **simple,** apparently atomic, eternal objects raises a question that divides process thinkers. Many of Whitehead's formulations seem to imply that there are a finite number of distinct shades of yellow. Hartshorne has insisted that colors are related to one another in continua, in which there is an infinite number of shades.. Puzzling conclusions can be drawn from either theory. Whitehead does not discuss this question.

NEXUS

In the **categories of existence** Whitehead pairs **subjective forms** and "**nexūs.**" Subjective forms are the way occasions **feel** the **past.** They are "**private matters of fact.**" Nexūs he identifies with "**public matters of fact.**"

A nexus is composed of multiple occasions that are together with one another. My desk is a nexus of molecular occasions, or, if there are no molecular or atomic occasions, of quanta of energy.

All the objects of ordinary experience are nexūs: sticks and stones, planets and stars, mountains and trees. So also are what we usually call **events.** But the denotation of the term extends even more widely. The air in the room and the atmosphere of the entire planet are both nexūs. So are the occasions that are together in an "**empty space.**" There is a nexus of all the occasions that constitute the entirety of the past of any occasion, that is, its **actual world.**

So extensive is the application of the term that it may be easier to understand it by identifying that to which it does not apply. First, a single occasion is not a nexus. A nexus is a plurality of occasions bound together by their internal relations. Second, a class or set, such as the set of all red objects, or the set of all poodles, is not a nexus. Internal relations among these entities do not enter into their identification as a class.

The idea of a nexus is very important for translating back and forth between Whitehead and most other philosophical systems. What many others call "actual entities," Whitehead calls "nexūs." This is most obvious in relation to philosophies that stay close to ordinary language and treat the objects of everyday experience as actual entities. But it is true also of most process philosophies, which take **events** as primary. Most of the events that are so treated are, for Whitehead, nexūs, that is, they are composed of multiple actual occasions.

A nexus functions, and therefore exists, in two ways. Whitehead calls them "**objective**" and "**formal.**" As objective the nexus exists for the observer. Tables and chairs are objective nexūs for human beings as are most of what in ordinary language we speak of as things or objects.

But the nexus consists of individual actual occasions, which do not exist only for observers. They exist also **formally** in themselves as processes of appropriating the **past** and thereby constituting themselves. A nexus also may be spoken of in terms of its **formal constitution.** There is much in the nexus formally that is not present for any one percipient subject **objectively**.

Whitehead sometimes distinguishes the **"initial data"** of an occasion from the **"objective datum."** The initial data constitute the prehended nexus **formally**, that is, with all the features of all the entities intact. The objective datum of the occasion as a whole is the way the new occasion prehends the nexus. Much of the richness of the nexus understood in the formal way is lost in its **objectification.**

This is also relevant for translation between Whitehead's philosophy and those of others. Some philosophers take an actual entity to be a nexus they experience as they experience it. Some want to go behind what the world is for observers to the world that is observed, as it is in itself, that is, to the nexus in its **formal** completeness.

SOCIETIES AND EMPTY SPACE

Societies are to **nexūs** much as actual occasions are to actual entities. Most of the nexūs we have considered are societies. That is, they have **"social order."** But there are also **"nonsocial"** nexūs, which means, nexūs with no social order.

The chief example of a **nexus** with no **social order** is found in **"empty space."** Empty space is not empty of actual occasions. In Whitehead's view something is going on everywhere, even in a vacuum. There is energy there. But in empty space nothing endures. Accordingly there is nothing that moves and nothing that can be measured. The relations of an occasion in empty space to earlier occasions are just as important to its existence as are relations to past occasions in the occasions that make up societies, but they do not generate social order. Empty space is space that is empty of societies.

Societies come into being when some characteristic of one occasion is inherited by other occasions. The continuance of that characteristic through time makes of the multiplicity of occasions that inherit and transmit this characteristic a "society." The members of a society have something in common, and unlike members of a set or class, they share this characteristic by virtue of their **feelings** of antecedent members of the same society. Societies endure through time, whereas actual occasions only occur and fade into the past. Accordingly, societies can change location, as individual actual occasions cannot. Measurement of how they function is possible.

Whitehead sometimes uses the term society when speaking of what we normally call human societies. A human being may belong to a variety of societies. He gives the example of persons who know Greek. They constitute a society because even though many of them do not know one another, they share a common characteristic derived from other members of the society. Many small towns or city neighborhoods are also societies, in that the members share characteristics derived from other members of the town or neighborhood.

However, Whitehead uses the term "society" more often in relation to nonhuman organisms, inanimate objects, or **nexūs** of **events.** These are of many varieties.

ENDURING OBJECTS OR PERSONALLY ORDERED SOCIETIES AND CORPUSCULAR SOCIETIES

Conceptually, the simplest form of **society** is one in which there is just one member at a time. Our own individual experience of ourselves is of this sort. One experience is followed by another and that by another, yet each is strongly connected to its predecessors. This is what is meant by a **personally ordered society.** In contrast to individual occasions in **empty space**, which we saw are lacking in **social order,** personal order constitutes a society that endures through **time.** It is, therefore, also called an **"enduring object."** Its endurance may be for a second or for a million years.

Although in its strictest definition, all enduring objects would be personally ordered societies, in Whitehead's actual usage, the term is sometimes used for macroscopic objects that endure even if the entities that are serially ordered are not actual occasions but **societies** of such entities. He refers to molecules as enduring objects. If we take his definition strictly, this would support the judgment that at any moment there is a single molecular occasion. But he also, at other points, indicates that molecules are **"structured societies."** One conclusion could be that Whitehead thought that a structured society could also be or have a unitary occasion. But it is more likely that Whitehead uses "enduring object" more loosely than his definition suggests.

Many of the physical objects with which we deal can be broken down into molecules. If we consider molecules to be enduring objects, then we can say that these ordinary physical objects can be analyzed into enduring objects. Whitehead calls these larger objects **"corpuscular societies."** Many of the objects that are, in other philosophies, taken as examples of *what is,* are, for Whitehead, "corpuscular societies." Rocks and gases and liquids are all corpuscular societies.

STRUCTURED SOCIETIES

Unfortunately for conceptual simplicity, neither living systems nor most of the smaller objects of scientific interest are as simple in their composition as **enduring objects** and **corpuscular societies**. A stone can be considered a corpuscular society of molecules, since these have much the same physical character even when separated from one another by the crushing of the stone. But the molecule cannot be similarly broken up into atoms. The structuring of the molecule goes beyond the co-existence of the atoms in it. The whole is quite different from the sum of its parts when the parts are considered in their separation from the whole. The molecule is thus a structured society rather than a corpuscular society. Presumably this is true of atoms as well, and probably of electrons and protons.

Whitehead defines a structured society as one that includes "**subordinate nexūs**" some of which are "**socially ordered**," and some are not. These latter are the **nonsocial nexūs** that we think of as **empty space**. The cell, as the unit of living things, is an especially interesting example of a structured society. Whitehead proposes a complex analysis here. The cell includes molecules which are themselves structured societies. In relation to the cell they are "**subordinate societies**." Like the molecules in a stone, they could exist independently of the cell. Whitehead focuses attention also on the empty space in the cell, the space that lacks any social order, considering this important for the behavior of the cell as a whole. This lack of social order makes novelty possible. It is here that Whitehead locates the life of the cell. This empty space constitutes a "**regnant nexus.**" Presumably it is "regnant" in the sense that the cell as a whole responds to stimuli in novel ways that these nexūs make possible.

The sharp distinction between the **societies** and the **nonsocial nexūs** is based on the teaching that social relations are constituted by repetition of forms. On this understanding, any novel element that may enter into a member of a society does not affect the society as a whole, that is, it is not repeated by successors. Since life is distinguished by novelty, it cannot be the property of a society. Hence it belongs to a nonsocial nexus and that means to the occasions in **empty space**.

However, this analysis was not Whitehead's last word. Apparently while he was working on the book, a new idea occurred to him. He did not go back and change what he had written, but this idea has proved particularly fruitful. However, for his fully developed understanding of living things, see below the discussion of "**living persons.**"

PREHENSION

I have with difficulty avoided using the term "**prehension**" thus far. The idea the term represents could not be avoided, and the term "**feeling,**" to be discussed below, has had to bear the weight. Prehension may be the single most important and original concept in Whitehead's philosophy.

A "prehension" consists in an **objective datum** as well as a **subjective form**. The objective datum is *what* it prehends. The subjective form is *how* it prehends it. In the simplest case, we have a prehension of a single actual occasion, so that the objective datum is the aspect of that occasion that is prehended. But the datum of most prehensions is a **nexus.** For example, especially in conscious experience, I prehend a stone, not the individual molecules of which if consists, much less the individual quanta. And the objective datum of the occasion as a whole is always a nexus, namely, the **actual world** of the occasion.

Prehensions are the way that what is *there* becomes something *here*. A prehension is the bond between two actual occasions. The past occasion shares in the constitution of the new occasion. From this perspective, we can say that something there becomes something here. This is the "**causal efficacy**" of the past occasion for the new one. Returning to the point of view of the new occasion, we can say that the new occasion draws the past occasion into itself. Thus one and the same relation can be viewed as the causal efficacy of the **past** or a prehension in the present.

A prehension is an **internal relation**. That is, it is internal to the prehending occasion while being external to the prehended occasion. The prehension does not change what it prehends, but the **subject** of the prehension becomes what it becomes through its prehensions. The relation is not symmetrical. The later occasion prehends and is thus partly constituted by the earlier one. The earlier occasions does not prehend and is not affected by the later on. Whitehead often speaks of the inter-relations among things. This is often literally true when the things in question are **societies.** For example, there are extensive interrelationships between plants and the animals that eat them. But as Hartshorne has made especially clear, no two occasions are symmetrically interrelated. Usually, one occasion is in the **past** of the other one. The relation between a present occasion and those in its past is never symmetrical. The past occasion exercises **causal efficacy** in the present one. The present occasion prehends the past one. This is Whitehead's view, but his language sometimes obscures the asymmetry of the relationship.

Although the overarching emphasis in Whitehead is on the occasion as **subject,** he sees that there is danger in using only this word. It gives the impression that the occasion is the only actor in its prehending of the **past.** Many interpreters have followed this lead, treating past occasions as the passive **data** out of which the new subject constructs itself.

To counter this image and emphasize the causal agency of antecedent occasions, Whitehead employs another term. He tells us that the occasion is the "**superject**" of its own prehensions. Its prehensions bring it into being. In other words, it does not first exist and then prehend the past. Its existence is constituted by its prehensions of the **past.** For the most part it is what the past occasions bring about in it.

There are many kinds of things that are prehended, and accordingly there are many types of prehensions. But what is most important for the student of Whitehead is to grasp the idea of prehending as such. Since it is not an idea that has been previously developed in the history of Western philosophy, it can only be grasped as an insight or a recognition of what is in fact taking place in all experience. In this section we will focus on communicating the general idea, reserving more technical discussion for later sections.

To gain a clearer sense of Whitehead's meaning one can consider one's own experience. What is the relation of one moment of experience to the preceding one? To a large extent it is a repetition or reenactment. What one was experiencing before still resonates in the present. It is felt now as something that was felt earlier.

An example may heighten the sense of how prehensions work. Suppose you are listening to music. You hear the final chord of a musical phrase. But why do you hear it as the final chord of a musical phrase? Is it a matter of consciously recalling past experiences? Obviously not. Unless the earlier occasions of experience are functioning in the present, there would simply be a succession of disconnected sounds. The past experience flows into the present. It does not constitute the present occasion of experience totally, because there must be the addition of the final chord. But the **past** is alive in the present. Still, one experiences the presence of the previous chords as derived from experiences in the past, the very recent past. This is an example of the prehension of the past experience by the now becoming experience. What was past becomes present, but it is present *as* derived from that past.

Prehension explains **causality** as well as immediate memory. It provides a way of understanding not only our relation to our own immediate **past,** but also our relation to our own bodies. In this relation, too, we have a vague but ineradicable sense of derivation. I know that I see *with* my eyes and hear *with* my ears. I also know that, when I have a toothache, the pain I feel derives from the pain in the tooth. Phenomenologically I cannot go much further, but if I combine elementary knowledge of physiology with my hard-won notion of prehension, I can develop plausible theories of how I prehend the neuronal occasions in the brain and, through them, **events** in other parts of the body.

This indicates the great importance of the body for Whitehead. Conscious experience misleads us in our philosophy by focusing on the relation of an external environment to us. This is quite understandable in evolutionary terms. For survival it is more important to attend to food and danger in the external environment than to the internal condition of the body. We attend to what we see rather than to the feeling of the eyes themselves. But without the prehension of the eyes there would be no visual experience of the outside world. It is a mistake to take patches of color as examples of the primary **data** of experience. Primary are past personal experiences and neuronal experiences. Secondary are other bodily experiences. The external world comes third. Nevertheless, it is important to recognize that we do prehend that world, too, not just patches of color but actual occasions that make up that world.

Whitehead can also explain quantum events in terms of prehensions. Obviously, quantum theory is both complex and unfinished. However, we may suppose that what occurs in one quantum **event** is largely determined by what has happened in other quantum events. Indeed its energy derives from the **past** and is transmitted to the **future.** The idea of prehension fits this objective knowledge about the quantum. The past enters into the present which then becomes part of the past that transmits to the future. The quantum comes into being as a unity of its prehensions of other quanta.

FEELING

The previous discussion dealt with only one type of **prehension,** the way one actual occasion participates in the constitution of another. Distinctions among types of such prehensions and more complex prehensions will be considered separately. But first we note that the very basic kind of prehension I have been describing can also be called a **"feeling."** Indeed, in sections preceding the introduction of prehensions, I spoke of feeling. The relation of "feeling" to "prehension" is much like the relation of actual occasion to actual entity. There is one kind of actual entity that is not an actual occasion, namely, **God**. Similarly, there is one kind of prehension that is not a feeling. It is called a "**negative prehension**." This is the exclusion of something from playing a role in the constitution of an actual occasion. The great majority of Whitehead's talk of prehensions is about "**positive prehensions**," prehensions through which something in the **past** is included in the constitution of the present occasion; so that the full identification of feelings with prehensions is only occasionally misleading.

Everything I have said about **prehension** in the preceding section applies to feeling, and everything I will say about feeling applies to prehension. I feel the occasions of my body and through them the external world. I feel my past experience. The quantum feels previous quanta.

The simplest example of a feeling is the feeling of a single actual occasion. Every feeling has a **datum.** The datum is, for that occasion, an "**object**"; so Whitehead calls it an "**objective datum**." But it is important to recognize that the objective datum, in this case, was, a moment ago, a **subject**. The objective datum is chiefly composed of feelings. The world is made up largely of feelings of feelings of feelings.

The **objective datum** is what the feeling feels, what is given to it, that is, its datum. A feeling also has a **"subjective form"**. This is how the datum is felt. It is feeling in the purely subjective sense rather than in the relational sense in which Whitehead uses the word.

In a few cases, part of the **subjective form** is **consciousness.** Other types of subjective forms are **purposes, valuations, adversions**, and **aversions**. But the predominant element in the subjective form of feeling is **emotion**. An actual occasion may be thought of chiefly as a throb of emotion, in the overwhelming majority of cases, nonconscious emotion. For the most part, therefore, an occasion emotionally feels the emotional feeling of antecedent occasions of the emotional feeling of their predecessors.

Going back to the musical illustration we may hear the chord of music with satisfaction or with disappointment, or with anticipation. One may downplay or "**value down**" the music, trying to turn attention to something else, or one may accent it or "**value up**," trying to overcome some distraction. In general one's **subjective form** of feeling in one moment repeats to a large extent the **subjective form** of feeling in the preceding moment, but change, even drastic change is possible.

At this point Whitehead engages in a bold speculation, which shows how serious he is about overcoming the dualism of the **objective** and **subjective** worlds. He affirms that what we know subjectively as **emotion** is measured objectively as energy. The emotional feeling of the emotional feeling of still another emotional feeling is described by physics as the vector transmission of energy.

SUBJECT AND SUPERJECT

When speaking of the individual entity that feels, Whitehead usually speaks of the actual occasion that feels as the "**subject.**" Indeed, much of the discussion of actual entities, actual occasions, prehensions, and feelings has been about subjects. When subjects are contrasted with objects, this is clarifying and important.

However, Whitehead recognizes that this language can also be misleading. We are accustomed to think of subjects as agents of action. To call an actual occasion a subject can easily give the impression that the becoming actual occasion already exists before it feels. Interpreters have sometimes so emphasized the action of the occasion in prehending the **past** that the past occasions appear as mere passive data awaiting this action. This is not Whitehead's vision.

For the most part the occasion and all its **prehensions** express the **causal efficacy** of past occasions. The prehensions are better understood as expressing their causal efficacy in the constitution of the new occasion, which only comes into being as these prehensions integrate in it. To capture this emergence of the new occasion out of the working of the past in it, Whitehead sometimes speaks of the new occasion as the "**superject.**"

If he tried to substitute superject for subject altogether, his vision would be falsified in an opposite way. It would become deterministic. The present would be seen as simply the outgrowth of the past. The term "subject" and the analysis of the activity of the subject in constituting itself out of the past are crucial. When Whitehead is most careful he speaks of the occasion as the subject/superject of its prehensions.

Whitehead also writes at times about the **superjective nature** of an occasion. There he has in mind the role of the occasion as operative in the constitution of other occasions. Just as an occasion needs to be seen as the superject of its own feelings, so also its role in constituting subsequent occasions should be recognized.

NEGATIVE PREHENSIONS

Feelings are **positive prehensions. "Negative prehensions"** are those that eliminate some items in the universe from being felt. They are the way actual occasions prehend most of the **eternal objects.** However, no past actual entity can be entirely eliminated in this way. All are felt or positively prehended. That means that it can never be for a new occasion as if there were total blank spots in its past. However, most of the feelings that constituted the actuality of most past entities *are* eliminated. For example, although the past includes the Roman Empire and all the events that made it up, most of the feelings of most of the actual occasions that occurred in that Empire have been eliminated from the **objective data** of occasions of human experience today.

Whitehead's formulations sometimes sound as though each occasion today **negatively prehends** all of that. Another understanding of his theory is that most of those feelings have been progressively eliminated from the **data** through generations of actual occasions. The negative prehensions in each occasion constitute the further elimination from feeling of additional elements of the past.

Since it is easy to understand that we feel only a very small part of the whole of the **past** as well as of the realm of **pure potentials**, one wonders why Whitehead makes as much as he does of **negative prehensions.** The answer is that he believes all the entities that make up the whole of the past, as well as all the **eternal objects,** are related. Every thing has some relevance to everything else, although this is graduated and fades off into negligibility. Given this connectedness, the failure to include something is not simply doing nothing. It is a positive act of exclusion. This act contributes to the **subjective form** of the new occasion.

There is an analogy that may be suggestive. In depth psychology there is a sense that everything that has happened to us is still with us even though we consciously remember very little of it. Some of our forgetting is an action on our part undertaken to avoid feelings of humiliation or shame. This is called repression. The facts or experiences that are repressed are excluded from direct participation in our current experience. But there is a strong **subjective form** associated with the act of their repression. Of course, in reality, the **subjective forms** of the vast majority of **negative prehensions** are trivial.

In any case, every occasion of human experience is confronted by more **data** than it can integrate. In order to assimilate new data from the environment it must exclude some of what it might inherit from its personal past. Without that exclusion novelty could not enter, but we should not minimize the loss. It is not hard to understand that such exclusion involves a **subjective form.**

CONCEPTUAL AND REVERTED PREHENSIONS OR FEELINGS

The previous discussion of feelings has had **physical feelings** in view. Physical feelings are **prehensions** of past occasions and **nexūs** of past occasion. But we noted earlier that in addition to actual occasions, there are also **eternal objects.** Some of these are also prehended positively or felt.

Conceptual feelings are prehensions of **eternal objects.** These are "**pure potentials.**" Many of these potentials are **ingredient** in what has been felt physically, but they become conceptual feelings only when they are distinguished from their actualization in what is physically felt and then felt in their distinct status as pure potentials. In this status they are valued as possibilities for actualization rather than as already ingredient in the past world. Accordingly, the **subjective form** of conceptual feelings is always **valuation,** so that conceptual feelings are also always "**conceptual valuations.**" Whitehead sometimes writes of "**appetitions.**" **Pure potentials** are never entertained neutrally. They are abstracted from the **physical prehension** for a reason.

Physical feelings and **conceptual valuations** are present in all actual occasions. For example, consider the prehension in one moment of your experience of a moment ago. There is a great deal of continuity, but the new experience does not reproduce the previous experience exactly. There is also change. Some features of the previous experience are intensified, others muted. Your physical feeling of the past occasion prehends the **subjective form** of the past occasion, that is, the **eternal objects** as they are **ingredient** in it. But the occasion also feels these **eternal objects** as **pure potentials** for reenactment in itself. Whitehead says that it sometimes values the eternal object that is the datum **up** and sometimes, **down.**

"**Conceptual reversions**" may or may not take place. A **reverted feeling** is of a possibility closely related to, but different from, the one that has been abstracted from the **physical prehensions** of past occasions. This introduces novelty. Of course, this same possibility may have been frequently actualized in the past. The vast majority of what is novel for an occasion in relation to the past it is prehending is not novel in the universe as a whole. But it does not enter the present experience through prehension of previous occasions in which it was **ingredient.** It enters because it is related to, but different from, what is given in the occasion's purely physical experience.

This is easily illustrated in human experience. Suppose I am irritated by something someone has said to me. In the next moment I feel my immediate **past** as irritated. My tendency is to reproduce that irritation. However, this is not a simply automatic process. I may distinguish that irritation as a *possibility* from the *actual* irritation derived from the past. I may **value** it somewhat negatively, in Whitehead's terminology, **down.** I may also become aware of alternative **emotions** that might clothe my feeling of the previous irritation. The **subjective form** of the prehension of the past irritation will no doubt continue to include irritation, but it may also include an element of embarrassment or shame for the exaggerated response to the stimulus. In a fairly short period of time, the actualization of possibilities received by reversion may alter the **subjective form** of my **physical feelings** considerably.

But why does Whitehead call this **"reversion"**? My guess is that he did so because he developed the idea first in relation to elementary physical phenomena. He comments that in our world reality consists more of "**vibratory**" phenomena than of sheer repetition by successive occasions. Vibration is the term he used for what are usually called waves. Perhaps he preferred this language because a vibration is an event that does not immediately imply a medium as would a wave. He understood vibrations to occur when a sequence of occasions alternates between two states. It changes from *a* to *b* and then reverts to *a*. Whitehead speculated that this alternation supported a greater "**intensity**" of emotion than would sheer repetition of form.

Clearly at the level of vibratory phenomena, the novelty introduced into the world by reversion is very slight. However, in human experience reversion can be cumulative. We will return to this topic when discussing **living persons**.

OBJECTIVE AND SUBJECTIVE SPECIES OF ETERNAL OBJECTS

Eternal objects function to objectify past actual entities and **nexūs** for new **subjects.** The **subjective form** of the new occasion is also characterized by eternal objects. Often the same eternal object functions to characterize both the **objective datum** and its subjective form. For example, in one moment I may feel the previous occasion of my experience as anxious. The subjective form of this feeling may well be anxiety. Anxiety belongs to the **"subjective species of eternal objects."**

There are other **eternal objects** that cannot characterize the **subjective form** of an occasion. The **objective datum** may be characterized by squareness, but the subjective form of seeing a square object cannot be squareness. Squareness, like mathematical forms generally, belongs to the **"objective species."**

There are still other **eternal objects,** however, that are harder to classify. For example, a given shade of yellow characterizes for me a **nexus** that makes up part of a painting. Can the **subjective form** of feeling this eternal object also be "yellow?" Surely not in a straightforward sense. The subjective form of one's experience cannot be yellow in the same sense that part of the painting is.

Nevertheless, Whitehead does not use colors as examples of **eternal objects** of the objective species. Apparently a color expresses something about the **nexus** it objectifies that can be reenacted in the percipient occasion. Charles Hartshorne developed a theory justifying this idea in his first book, *The Philosophy and Psychology of Sensation.* He affirms an **emotional** quality that can be expressed alike through various sensa and that can be shared by the human experience and the perceived world. In *Adventures of Ideas* Whitehead suggests that we rightly live with a basic faith that there is real continuity between appearance and reality. That would mean here, that there is an emotional continuity between the colors of things and their **subjective forms.**

INGRESSION OF ETERNAL OBJECTS

Eternal objects characterize actual occasions. Apart from this characterization there can be no actualities at all. Although the actual occasion is never exhausted by the eternal objects that characterize it, it is actualized only in and through their realization.

Whitehead describes this process as eternal objects becoming **ingredients** in actual occasions. This ingredience may be in their data, for example as visual qualities, or in their **subjective forms**, as emotions, or in both. This becoming ingredient he names **"ingression."**

To say that an eternal object ingresses into an actual occasion may give the impression of action on its part. There is none. Eternal objects do not act. The action is that of actual entities.

RESTRICTED AND UNRESTRICTED INGRESSION OF ETERNAL OBJECTS

Initially, the **eternal object** has **ingression** either in *what* is prehended, the **objective data** of experience, or in *how* it is experienced, that is, the **subjective form** of the experience. If I see a blue carpet, the quality of blue has **"unrestricted"** **ingression** into the occasions of my experience. Similarly if I feel uneasy, the quality of uneasiness has unrestricted ingression. These modes of unrestricted ingression were discussed earlier.

But an **eternal object** can also be the **datum** of a **conceptual feeling.** Conceptual feelings may be integrated with **physical feelings** in various ways. Through **reversion** they may also lead to other conceptual feelings and be integrated with them in very complex patterns in human thought. Whitehead calls the **ingression** of eternal objects as data of **conceptual prehensions** or feelings or of thought **"restricted ingression."** If a mathematician is thinking of the properties of an equilateral triangle, this triangular shape and the properties recognized in it have restricted ingression in the actual occasions of the mathematician's experience. If she is looking at a triangular object, the ingression is unrestricted.

THE PHYSICAL AND MENTAL (OR CONCEPTUAL) POLES

Physical feelings are feelings of actual occasions. They provide the basis for the development of every new actual occasion. But all occasions also have **conceptual feelings** or feelings of **potentialities.** The simplest of these are feelings of **pure potentials** or **eternal objects**. These are conceptual feelings. There are also combinations of physical and conceptual feelings.

In much of modern philosophy the physical and the mental have been drastically separated. Descartes taught us to think of them as metaphysically different. For Whitehead, it would be misleading to ignore the difference, but this difference should be recognized as two aspects of every occasion, every **nexus,** every **society,** and every event. It is not a basis for distinguishing two types of entities.

This means, emphatically, that Whitehead rejects metaphysical dualism. But this does not mean that he denies differences between mentality and physicality. Every occasion includes both physicality and mentality. To say this is not dualism but **dipolarity.** Whitehead occasionally speaks instead of "**bipolarity.**" The occasion can be divided in thought into a "**physical pole,**" consisting of its **physical feelings** and a **conceptual** or **mental pole,** consisting in its **conceptual feelings**. In this division all the more complex forms of feeling that integrate the physical and the conceptual feelings are considered as part of the mental or **conceptual pole.**

There are occasions in which mentality plays a very small role. There are other occasions in which mentality is the dominant factor. There are still other occasions that lie between these extremes. The extremes help us understand how dualistic thinking arose, but they do not justify it. **Dipolar** thinking is basic to Whitehead's whole philosophy.

SIMPLE (CAUSAL) PHYSICAL FEELINGS AND TRANSMUTED FEELINGS

The original discussion of **prehension** and feeling above focused on **simple feelings.** They are also called "**causal.**" One occasion feels the emotion of the previous occasion and thus appropriates it. There is an energy flow from one to the next. This is the basis of causality in the world.

This is an important point. For the most part modern philosophy since Hume has had difficulty with the idea of one event as actually, or causally, being affected by another event. Hume showed that if one takes sense experience as the only direct access to an external world, common sense and scientific ideas of **causality** can not be justified. Kant responded that the human mind necessarily organizes experience in causal terms. In either case, we can say nothing about causal relations in the world as it is in itself, apart from the constructions of the human mind, but we have no choice but to think in these terms with respect to what appears to us. Much of the philosophical discussion is still caught between the sensory empiricism of Hume and the constructive idealism of Kant. Whitehead's claim that actual occasions participate in constituting other actual occasions changes the conversation radically. In his view occasions participate by being the **data** of **causal feelings** that jointly constitute much of the new occasion. We know that there is causality in the world because it plays so large a role in the constitution of all our experiences.

Nevertheless, most human feelings are not of the type that Whitehead calls causal. They do not have as their **data** individual actual occasions. We live in a socially-ordered world. It is comprised of mountains and oceans and buildings and trees and flowers. We do not experience any of these in terms of the myriads of quanta that make them up. We experience them as large, relatively well unified, objects. This is clearly true in the case of the objects of sensation. But it is also true in our experience of our own bodies. Even in a tooth ache, it is the tooth as a whole that aches, not the quantum **events,** or even the individual cellular events, which make them up. Whitehead needs to explain why our actual experience of the world is so different from what the **simple physical feelings** alone would produce.

Whitehead describes the change from the many simple feelings of microscopic entities to the experience of large objects as **"transmutation."** The same **eternal object** is abstracted from the many individual occasions and is then applied to all of them. The **society** composed of many occasions is then felt as one entity. Most philosophy takes the data of **transmuted feelings** as the clue to reality in general or, at least, to physical reality. Whitehead does not, but this in no way minimizes the importance of transmuted feelings.

Pure and Hybrid Physical Prehensions or Feelings

Up until this point we have been considering primarily **"pure physical feeling."** Pure physical feelings are feelings of the physical feelings of antecedent occasions. These are the **causal feelings** that transmit energy from occasion to occasion. However there is another kind of physical feeling. It is also a feeling of an antecedent occasion. But it feels that occasion's **conceptual feeling**, not its **physical feeling.**

Whitehead did not have this possibility in mind while writing much of *Process and Reality.* He thought of **physical feelings** as transmitting energy and constituting causal relations. They explained the stability of the world. The all-important **social order** they made possible was also an expression of commonality and repetition. He argued, for example, that personal identity is a matter of repeating some unchanging pattern throughout life and that the novelty in cellular responses to stimuli depends on there being a **nonsocial nexus** in the **empty spaces** of the cell. The point was that **social order** as such is incompatible with originality of response.

Once Whitehead recognized that **physical prehensions** could have

conceptual prehensions as their **data,** he had a new way of understanding cells and of persons as well as much else. The novelty introduced into one occasion by **reversion** can be transmitted to the next. The novel feeling of that past occasion becomes part of the physical prehension of the new occasion and can be transmitted to future occasions through pure physical prehensions. If novel feelings in one moment could not be felt thereafter by **hybrid prehensions,** they could have no continuing effect. But in fact we know that animals learn. In Whitehead's language, the **conceptual feeling** of one occasion is channeled or "**canalized**" in future occasions through the agency of a hybrid feeling.

The distinction between hybrid feelings and pure physical ones is helpful in other ways as well. Whitehead emphasizes that the whole past or actual world of an occasion plays a role in its constitution. In his formulations it is not always clear whether he means that the more distant **past events** are mediated to the present entirely through their successors. Sometimes it is quite explicit that the relation can be unmediated as well. But problems arise if we suppose that energy can be transmitted from a past occasion to successors more that once.

Late in his writing of the book, Whitehead proposes that **pure physical prehensions** probably depend on spatio-temporal connection. The **causal efficacy** of the more distant past is mediated by intermediate events. On the other hand, hybrid physical prehensions do not depend on such contiguity. The contemporary emphasis on the transmission of information fits well with his idea of hybrid prehensions. He would probably understand the growing evidence in physics of the entanglement of distant occasions also in these terms. He explicitly indicates the explanatory role of hybrid feelings in psychic phenomena.

LIVING PERSON

Humanistic and religious readers of Whitehead often complain that the human being disappears into the matrix of minuscule actual entities. This is a misreading. Whitehead does believe that minuscule actual entities, occasions of quantum action, are very important for cosmology. But he is equally clear that moments of human experience are not analyzable into these **events.** Indeed they are not divisible into smaller actual entities at all. Human experience is taken as it is, nonreductively. Because a moment of human experience has the status of being an actual occasion, its **causal efficacy** cannot be ignored, as is typically done in the sciences.

Far from losing the human in the matrix of quantum events, he takes its full actuality as the starting point of much of his philosophical analysis.

Nevertheless, prior to his development of the idea of **hybrid feelings**, his concept of the person was impoverished. A person was a **personally ordered society** of actual occasions. But personal order simply implied that there was a serial sequence of occasions each of which inherited from its predecessor a common character. Electrons and molecules qualified equally with human beings as personally ordered societies. All could be equally well named "**enduring objects**."

In other words, Whitehead up to that point understood **personal order** as a form of **social order**, and he defined the latter in terms of derivation of a common form from antecedent members of the group. **Hybrid prehensions** introduced the possibility of a new kind of **society**. Since he did not redefine "society" to take account of this, we might have to say that a **living person** is not a society. I prefer to say that it is a different kind of society, but that would require providing a broader definition. While there certainly are societies with personal order that transmit the same form from occasion to occasion, there are other societies with personal order that are alive. The transmissions from occasion to occasion in these societies introduce novelty.

These **societies** are unquestionably found in animals with central nervous systems. The brains of these animals give rise to a unified experience that is quite different from the addition of all the neuronal experiences that contribute to it. As humans, we know this experience as most intimately who we are. Whitehead called these momentary experiences "**final percipient occasions**" or "**dominant occasions**." The sequence of these occasions he called a "**living person.**"

Living persons like other **personally ordered societies** do inherit elements of common form from their predecessors through their **pure physical feelings**. But they also inherit from their predecessors' **conceptual prehensions**. Among the conceptual feelings there are some that simply repeat elements of the **past,** but there are others that have introduced novelty. The antecedent occasion may have gained information not present in its predecessors. The new occasion, through its **hybrid prehensions** may appropriate this new information. It may add further to it. In other words, in living persons there is learning.

The emergence of novelty of this kind does not leave what has been repeated from the past alone. The integration of the two changes both.

Over time there may be little common element of form. There may be little common element of form between a girl of three and the woman she has become at sixty. But this does not mean that she is not the same living person. The occasions that make up the **living person** sum up the ever growing past rather than simply repeat it. In *Adventures of Ideas* Whitehead shifts from "living person" to the more traditional language of **"soul."**

A question that is raised in many contexts about human persons is their embodiment. Some argue that a person is his or her body. Platonic and Cartesian philosophy separates the person as **soul** sharply from the body. Whitehead's view lies between these poles. Strictly speaking, the person is distinct from the body. As the soul or psyche, it is not as such the bodily organism. We can speak both the "person" and of the "psycho-physical organism," which includes the person and the body.

But Whitehead throughout his philosophy emphasizes that each actual entity, or each **event,** is largely constituted by its relations to, or **prehensions** of, antecedent events. The **final percipient occasion** is largely constituted by what it perceives, although it integrates these perceptions into a single pattern. To a large extent, the living person sums up what is taking place in the body and functions for the sake of the well being of the body. Further, it is important to remember that whereas in Plato and Descartes the **soul** is metaphysically different from the body, for Whitehead it is not. The body is composed of occasions of experience, the soul or living person is also composed of occasions of experience. There are distinctions, but there is certainly no dualism.

Followers of Whitehead discuss where else living persons are to be found other than somewhere in the brains of animals with central nervous systems. Probably the chief candidate is the unicellular organism. Whitehead himself cracks the door to this hypothesis without clearly walking through it. For Whiteheadians, such questions are to be decided by evidence. Most Whiteheadians now think the evidence that unicellular organisms learn suffices for us to affirm that they are living persons.

Whitehead depicts the occasions that make up the **living person** as flitting around in the interstices of the brain surrounded by a **nonsocial nexus**. His language here seems connected with the way he thought of living persons before the introduction of **hybrid feelings**. However, it is the only speculation he offers.

PURE AND IMPURE CONCEPTUAL PREHENSIONS OR FEELINGS (PROPOSITIONAL FEELINGS)

Thus far we have contrasted **pure physical feelings** with **hybrid** ones. In this section we contrast **"pure" conceptual feelings** with **"impure"** or **"propositional"** feelings. Occasionally Whitehead speaks of **"pure"** feelings without making clear which contrast he has in mind. The reader should be warned, but not troubled. This double use of "pure" causes few problems. The context usually makes clear what is meant.

A pure **conceptual** feeling is the feeling of an **eternal object** as such. This was the only form of conceptual feeling that we had in view in the section on this topic above.

The contrast here is with an **"impure conceptual feeling,"** which Whitehead sometimes says can equally well be considered an **impure physical prehension**. This is also called a **"propositional feeling."** Its **datum** is the "**contrast**" of the datum of a conceptual feeling with that of an "**indicative feeling**," that is, a physical feeling stripped of its actual characteristics. This contrast is a "**proposition**," which is also known as an "**impure potential for the specific determination of matters of fact**," in distinction from an **eternal object,** which is a **pure potential.**

PROPOSITION

A **proposition** is defined very much as an **eternal object** is. The difference is that an eternal object is a *pure* potential and a proposition is an *impure* potential. An eternal object is disconnected from actuality; a proposition is tied to it. Propositions come into being along with actualities. Eternal objects do not. They are strictly timeless.

The use of the term **"proposition"** suggests a connection with logic. Whitehead emphasizes that propositions play a vast role in experience beyond the one they play in logic, but logic may be a good place to begin. We can start with a common statement, such as "The dog is brown." "The dog" refers us to what Whitehead would describe as a very complex "**society**" of "actual occasions." "Brown" refers us to an "**eternal object**." The statement brings these together.

Now we note that, for Whitehead, the statement points us to a **potential**. The **potential** is not the statement but the dog itself as brown. **Propositions** exist in the real world as what Whitehead describes as "**lures for feeling**." Some of the propositions are realized in the world, some are not. The latter may be called **false**, but "false" propositions may be more important than **true** ones. For example, they may describe the way things *should* be and move us to action.

This fairly common-sense understanding of **propositions** gives way in Whitehead to a more precise and powerful one. The problem with the statement "The dog is brown." is that the **logical subject** already contains descriptors. Suppose what we thought was a dog was in fact a wolf. Judging such a proposition then becomes difficult. The more precise statement of the proposition is "*That* or *it* is doggy and brown." "That" or "it" simply indicates the entity about which we want to speak, the **logical subject** of the proposition. One connects to that entity, whatever it may be, certain **eternal objects**, which Whitehead calls the "**predicative pattern**." One is holding up the possibility that they characterize that object. The note of **potentiality** remains, but the **prehension** of the **predicative pattern** is tied to or integrated with the prehension of a particular entity.

This is different, however, from simply integrating a "**physical**" and a "**conceptual feeling**." Another kind of abstraction has taken place. The "**physical feeling**" was of "actual entities" with many complex characteristics. The "**proposition**" does not integrate that **prehension** with the prehension of "**eternal objects**." Instead it strips the "physical feeling" of all the "eternal objects" that characterized its **datum**. What is left, Whitehead says, is an "**indicative feeling**." It is this indicative feeling that is integrated with the conceptual feeling. That integration provides us with the prehension of an "**impure potential**," that is, with an impure or propositional feeling.

Perceptive and Imaginative Propositions

There are two main types of **proposition, "perceptive"** and **"imaginative."** Their difference can be easily understood in a general way. In a perceptive proposition, the **predicative pattern** that is attributed to the **logical subject** is one that has been derived from the actual occasions that were **physically prehended** and from which the **logical subject** was also derived. If the **physical feeling** was of a brown dog, and the proposition associates brownness and dogginess with the logical subject, then we have a perceptive proposition. If, instead, we think of what we are seeing as a cat or as black, we have an imaginative proposition.

However, this simple formulation must be qualified in a variety of ways. For example, strictly speaking, the issue is not whether the **predicative pattern** is the same as the one of which the **physical feeling** was stripped, but whether it was derived from that **physical prehension**. The same predicative pattern could have been derived from previous experience, for example. The **physical feeling** from which it was derived is then called the "**physical recognition**." Obviously, if the physical recognition is different, the likelihood is that the **predicative pattern** is also different, so that we would have a simple case of an imaginative proposition. But it *could* be the same. That would not make the proposition perceptive.

It might seem that a perceptive proposition must be **true.** But this is not the case. In fact, in the case of the brown dog, the reality is much more complex. There are **reversions** at various stages, in the **events** making up the dog and also in the transmission of light to us, and finally in the move from **perception in the mode of causal efficacy** to **perception in the mode of presentational immediacy**. In the case of visual experience, this would always occur. Whitehead believes there is a real connection between what we see and how it appears to us, but there are also great differences between the actual characteristics of the things we see and the predicative pattern we project on them in **presentational immediacy.** The fact that we have a perceptive proposition in no way guarantees accuracy.

Far fewer **reversions** are involved when the **proposition** is about one's own past experience rather than an external object. Here there is no necessity of reversion. One might perceive that one's earlier experience included enjoyment of the taste of food. If no reversion is present, the perceptive feeling would be "authentic" and the proposition would be **"true."**

An **imaginative proposition** could also be **true.** The difference is that nothing about the way it arises can give any reason to believe it is true. Scientific hypotheses are typically imaginative propositions. Some of them become very well established theories. But this is based on complex tests rather than the evidence of immediate experience.

Truth

The idea of **truth** has had difficulty in recent philosophy. Traditionally truth has been understood as the correspondence to reality of what is said or written or thought. However, much philosophy now lacks the idea of an independent reality to which language or thought could correspond. Even if such a reality exists, there seems, to many philosophers, to be no way to know it. If we are blankly ignorant with regard to reality, it would be meaningless to declare that a statement about it is true or **false.** And finally, language and thought are not the sorts of things that could correspond with a reality that is not constituted of language or thought.

Reflection of this sort has led many of those who still want to speak of **"truth"** to turn to coherence views of truth. An idea will be accepted as true if it coheres with other well-accepted ideas that have stood the test of time. Others offer pragmatic views of truth. One accepts an idea as true if the consequences of accepting it are positive. I will believe there is truly a gap in the wall at a certain point if, when guided by that belief, I succeed in walking through the wall.

Whitehead recognizes the importance of coherence and of pragmatic results in the effort to determine what is **true.** However, his definition of truth returns to correspondence. As we have seen he believes that we live in a real world composed of actual occasions. Accordingly, the first objection listed above carries no weight. He believes that we prehend these actual occasions; so the second objection is not an obstacle. However, he agrees that language and thought are not the sorts of things that can correspond to this real world.

For this reason it is very important to recall that a **proposition**, for Whitehead, is not a species of language. Language usually calls attention to propositions, but there is never a one-to-one correspondence between language and any particular proposition. A proposition is the way some actual occasion or **nexus** of actual occasions may be. If the actual occasion in fact exists in just that way, then the **proposition** is **true.** The correspondence is not between language or thought and reality; it is between how something may be and how it is.

We have seen in the previous section that **prehension** may directly provide truth if there are no **reversions** involved. This leaves open the question as to how one can know that there are no **reversions** involved. Hence, the **belief** that some prehensions provide true information about the real world provides no assurance that any claim or belief to have such truth is justified. Other tests are needed to justify any claim to truth, and no test is ever final and certain. The affirmation that there is truth does not provide certainty about what it is

On the other hand, **belief** that some **propositions** are true does make the quest for truth meaningful. Many claimants to truth can be refuted. Others withstand efforts at refutation. Some of these are highly illuminating. For practical purposes we may have considerable confidence that we are close to the truth on many matters.

The connection between truth and language remains important. People want to express what they take to be truth in language. That means, in Whitehead's understanding, that they want to find language that directs attention to true **propositions**. At best, however, the language will elicit a cluster of propositions that overlap in large part with the propositions the speaker or writer has in mind. There will never be complete identify between the two clusters.

The problem is that the language does not fully control what **propositions** are elicited by it. The best scenario is the one mentioned in the preceding paragraph, one in which what one says or writes evokes into feeling propositions that extensively overlap with those one intends. Usually communication is less accurate. Some of the propositions elicited may be markedly different from the intention of the writer or speaker. This is as true of Whitehead's writings as of any others. I am trying to elicit propositions in the reader that correspond with propositions intended by Whitehead. The best I can hope for is considerable overlap.

Although truth is important for Whitehead, on more than one occasion he affirms that it is more important that a **proposition** be interesting than that it be true. Clearly a **"false" proposition** may lure us to change a bad situation or to invent something that is needed. Expanding the imagination may be more important than determining the exact situation in the past. We want to evoke attention to important and relevant propositions and to do so in a way that elicits response. That is why "interest" is crucial.

Still, truth adds to interest. Pure fantasy recognized as such can be briefly entertaining, but a relevance assured by the inclusion of truth renders ideas more interesting. Truth retains its importance.

In addition to the general question of how there can be correspondence between **propositions** and reality, there is a specific question about how there can be truth about the **past.** Since Whitehead holds that the past is **objectively immortal,** the solution given above to the general question covers some of this. A **proposition** about Napoleon's plans at a particular time may correspond, or fail to correspond with what Napoleon planned at that time.

But many statements by historians cannot be dealt with so easily. Consider a discussion of the relative amount of wheat harvested in France and Germany in the first decade of the nineteenth century. With what **past events** could statements of this sort correspond? Yet surely some

propositions on this topic are closer to truth than others. For this to be so, the truth must exist. Whitehead asserts that the truth is the way all things are together in **God**. The statements of historians can more or less correspond to this. Of course, this gives little guidance as to how to determine which propositions are closer to the truth. It only explains how the claim to truth can be meaningful.

INTELLECTUAL FEELINGS AND PHYSICAL PURPOSES AS GENERIC CONTRASTS

Contrasts are of great importance in the construction of actual occasions. Many contrasts are of diverse **nexūs** and actual occasions. That is they are integrations of physical feelings. But there are also contrasts of actual occasions with **potentials, pure** and **impure**. Since we could consider actuality and potentiality as different genus, Whitehead calls these **"generic contrasts."** We will consider first the generic contrast of the **propositions** discussed in the preceding section with actual occasions. The prehensions of these contrasts are **"intellectual feelings."** We will then note that there are far simpler generic contrasts between **eternal objects** and actual occasions. Whitehead calls the prehension of these **"physical purposes."**

The **propositional feeling** strips **the physical feeling** bare of all its characteristics, transforming it into an **indicative feeling** before integrating it with the **conceptual feeling** of its **predicative pattern**. Accordingly, a further level of integration is still needed. Above we used "*it* as doggy and brown' as an example of a proposition. This must be compared with what was physically felt. That is to say, the propositional feeling must be integrated with the physical feeling from which the indicative feeling of the **logical subject** was derived. This integration gives us our ordinary perception of the brown dog. Whitehead calls it an **"intellectual feeling."**

That may seem far fetched. Don't we just see the brown dog to start with? Whitehead thinks not. In order to perceive we have to distinguish what is from what is not. He calls this the "**affirmation/negation contrast.**" We have to recognize that things might be other than they are. If one had never experienced any color except one shade of brown, it would be very difficult to perceive the dog as brown. It is because one implicitly perceives that the dog is not black or white that one is aware of the brownness.

This type of intellectual feeling is a **"conscious perception."** The **propositional feeling** that it integrates with the physical feeling is explained in the section above as a **perceptive feeling.** In a perceptive feeling the **logical subject** of the **proposition** that is felt and its **predicative pattern** derive from the same physical feeling. That is, the **eternal objects** that constitute dogginess and brown arise from the same physical feeling as the "it" that is stripped of its felt characteristics. I consciously perceive a brown dog.

The **propositional feeling** that is integrated with the **physical feeling** may also be an **imaginative feeling.** In this case, the **predicative pattern** is derived from some other source than the **physical feeling** that provides the **logical** subject. This type of **generic contrast** is called an "**intuitive judgment**." Part of the **subjective form** of an **intuitive judgment** will be "**belief**," "**disbelief**," or "**suspended judgment**." For example, the predicative pattern may be softness and furrines. That is I may be imagining that the dog is furry and soft based on my experience with other, somewhat similar dogs. I may judge that this is the case or that it is not the case. Or I may simply wonder.

This analysis applies to conscious experiences generally. What enables them to be conscious is the comparison of what is with what may be. As we have seen, this requires a complex process of abstraction from what is and then comparing some **proposition** about how that entity might be with the way it was initially felt. A high-grade occasion, such as an animal experience, can come to completion in that kind of intellectual feeling.

It takes this **affirmation/negation contrast** to attain to **consciousness,** and this happens only with **intellectual feeling.** Does this mean that all elements of an experience in which consciousness plays a role are unified in intellectual feelings? Whitehead assumes not. Most of our feelings of the neurons in our brain are not dealt with in this elaborate way. None of those **prehensions** are conscious.

How else then can feelings be integrated? Whitehead describes the alternative form of closure as "**physical purposes.**" These are like **propositional feelings** except that they move directly to the integration of the **physical** and the **conceptual feeling** without going through the stage of **indicative** and propositional feelings. They compare the **eternal object** abstracted from the data of the physical feeling (or perhaps a **reverted feeling**) with the **objective data** of the physical feeling. The prehended occasions exercise their **causal efficacy** through this integration. What we actually experience derives much from these neurons. But we are never conscious of them. The relation is quite simply cause and effect, although we then integrate these numerous physical purposes with the **intellectual feelings** in a final **satisfaction**.

What then about the quanta? Does the experience that is a quantum event resemble ours sufficiently to justify calling it an "experience" at all? Whitehead thinks so. He thinks the quanta also have physical purposes. They achieve what intensity is possible for them by integrating **conceptual** and **physical feelings**. This does not introduce them to the level of the **affirmation/negation contrast**. They have no **propositional feelings**. They are not conscious. Since they resemble only the part of our experience that is not conscious, those who identify experience with conscious experience will oppose extending the term "experience" to them. For Whitehead, however, **consciousness** is a **subjective form** of some of the **prehensions** of high-grade occasions of experience. In no way does it delimit experience as such. What happens in the process of self-constitution of a quantum occasion is the same as what happens in much of ours.

Perception in the Modes of Causal Efficacy and Presentational Immediacy

Conscious perception, we saw, is the integration of a **propositional feeling** with a physical one. This can be perception of one's own past experience. But for the most part **conscious perception** is our experience of our environment. Much of it is visual. The analysis of how we perceive our world in this sense is somewhat more complex.

It, too, begins with **physical feeling**. In the case of visual experience, this feeling is of something external to the body. It is, of course, highly mediated. **Events** somewhere in the room, for example, reflect light toward my eye, where it is transformed into stimuli that are transmitted through the nerves to the occipital lobe of my brain. I abstract from this some **eternal object** which I then project back onto the **region** of space which reflected the light to me a fraction of a second earlier. I see that contemporary region of space as a patch of color.

Actually, however, that is not quite true. I see it as a colored wall. In other words, I integrate **transmuted physical feeling** of the actual occasions that make up the wall with my **conceptual feeling** of a given color. What was lacking in the other account was the highly mediated character of the **physical feeling** from which the **eternal object** projected on the wall is abstracted.

The impact of the **events** in that relatively remote **region** upon me is what Whitehead calls **"perception in the mode of causal efficacy."** I derive feelings from the occipital lobe which derived them from the eye, which derived them from the light reflected by that part of the wall. But when I abstract a color from my experience it appears to me as there now. What relation it has to the events that were **causally efficacious** for me is hard to fathom. But that I now see that region of space as having a certain color is indubitable. That I actually experience the color as characterizing the wall is also hard to dispute, although drawing conclusions from that about what is really there is quite risky. In any case, Whitehead calls the integration of the **propositional feeling** and the **physical prehension** a **conscious perception.**

What is most important about this account is that it dethrones the primacy of **perception in the mode of presentational immediacy.** A great deal of philosophy has assumed that this, and only this, is our access to the external world. For a long time the philosophers followed common sense in attributing the **eternal object** not merely to a spatial locus but also to the physical object located there, such as the wall. They thought of themselves as seeing people and houses and horses, rather than patches of color. But as they became more rigorous, they concentrated purely on presentational immediacy, that is, on what was immediately given as sense data. In that mode we receive only the appearances or phenomena, and that means only the **eternal objects.**

Whitehead agreed that in the pure mode of presentational immediacy we experience only the phenomena. But he emphasized that this pure mode is derivative from perception in the mode of causal efficacy. This consists of **physical feelings**, and physical feelings are what relate us to actual occasions other than ourselves in the present moment.

This analysis of experience is of great philosophical importance. Many philosophers have come to assume that, on an empirical basis, we cannot affirm the reality of a world beyond our sensory experience. This has led many philosophers to move farther and farther away from common sense. For them we are either left in our own private worlds of experience or are obliged to conclude that we construct the world rather than discovering it. For Whitehead the common sense view is correct. We know there is a world beyond ourselves because we experience it as such. Of course, common sense can lead to naïve views about that world that Whitehead does not share. Whitehead's understanding of that world is shaped by physics, which teaches that the actuality is quite different from the way it appears to us. But the external world possesses the actuality that common sense assumes, and Whitehead speculates that what is felt as there and what is actually there have some real connection.

Symbolic Reference

The integration **of propositional** and **physical feelings** described in the discussion of perception above entails **"symbolic reference."** The **eternal object** or **predicative pattern** given in **perception in the mode of presentational immediacy** is referred to the actual occasions or **societies** that are given in **perception in the mode of causal efficacy**. Hence ordinary sensory perception can be called **perception in the mode of symbolic reference.**

In Whitehead's view what many philosophers treat as the most basic form of **perception** already involves symbolism. This indicates the extreme importance of symbolism in his thought. Clearly perception is by no means the only example. All language involves symbols and their reference. A word may be the symbol for other words which can equally be symbols for it. A word can also be a symbol for a physical object such as a tree, but a tree can also be the symbol that refers one to the word. There are also nonlinguistic symbols, such as a flag or incense used in a religious service.

Experience is symbolic through and through.

On the other hand, it is equally significant that Whitehead speaks chiefly of **symbolic reference.** Since this reference is often to entities that are *actual* we do not end up in idealism or in a world composed exclusively of symbols. Many philosophers have made the "linguistic turn," arguing that language is really all that we have and that one bit of language can refer only to other bits of language. Whitehead makes strong statements about the importance of language, and much of language functions primarily as symbolic reference to other bits of language. This glossary is largely a matter of such references of terms to other terms. However, in explaining terms I frequently ask readers to relate them to nonlinguistic aspects of their experience. If these references fail, from a Whiteheadian point of view, the whole program collapses.

Not only can language symbolically refer beyond language, but also nonlinguistic entities such as actual occasions and **societies** also function as symbols. Further, while they function in the experience of perceivers as symbols, they have their own actuality independently of this function, and they function causally as well as symbolically. The world is not limited to symbols.

THE SUBJECTIVIST PRINCIPLE AND THE REFORMED SUBJECTIVIST PRINCIPLE

A great deal of modern Western philosophy has adopted what Whitehead calls **"the subjectivist principle."** This takes experience in the mode of **presentational immediacy** as primary. When it is taken this way, sensation becomes the fundamental element in primary experience. Whitehead identifies the view that the bare reception of the sensa is the basis of all experience as the "**sensationalist principle.**"

The **subjectivist principle** is very similar. It assumes that the experienced **datum** is as it is given in **presentational immediacy**. That means that it can be analyzed fully in terms of **eternal objects**. There is nothing else there. When this principle is accepted, the sensationalist doctrine turns the entire world into nothing but appearance or phenomena.

Whitehead rejects both of these principles. Occasions are not passive recipients of sensations but active producers of these. They clothe their sensations in **subjective forms** partly derived from the **eternal objects** by which they objectify the data and partly by the underlying **perception in the mode of causal efficacy**.

Furthermore, the data of experience are primarily the actual occasions felt in the **mode of causal efficacy**. It is these, rather than the **eternal objects** with which **presentational immediacy** objectifies them, that constitute the **actual world**. Thus Whitehead breaks drastically from the tradition in which these principles play so prominent a role.

Nevertheless, he is also a subjectivist. His subjectivist principle is **"reformed."** His doctrine is that apart from **subjects** there is nothing at all. There are no objects where there are no subjects to objectify them. This is true also for **eternal objects** and the **extensive continuum**. Potentiality does not exist apart from actuality. The difference between Whitehead's **"reformed subjectivist principle"** and the "subjectivist principle" he opposes is that the world is constituted primarily by present subjects prehending other subjects, not by subjects prehending only eternal objects.

THE ONTOLOGICAL PRINCIPLE

When we seek to explain the world including perception and symbolism, we cannot begin with **eternal objects.** They describe but they do not explain. The **reason** any occasion becomes what it does is to be sought in actual entities. The **ontological principle** is that only actual entities act; only they are the **reasons** for what happens.

This may seem too obvious to need articulation. But in fact, many explanations take a different form. Scientists often "explain" by appeals to "laws." An **event** is said to happen as it does because it obeys the laws of physics. This is often a convenient expression, and it may point in the right direction. But it is also misleading, and it too often encourages reasoning that commits the **fallacy of misplaced concreteness**. "Laws" are generalization or abstractions. They do not have **causal efficacy**. They cannot act. They are not the "**reasons**" for anything. Individual occasions do not obey them. A full and adequate explanation must trace the **cause** or reason for every feature of every occasion to some actual entity.

Stated in this form, the ontological principle could be understood to lead to complete determinism. If everything in a concrescing occasion is explained by the actual entities in its **actual world**, then, the outcome of the actual occasion is fully predetermined. For Whitehead, however, the concrescing occasion itself is part of its own **reason**. It, too, makes a **decision**, so that exactly what an occasion becomes is finally determined by the occasion itself. This is in accord with the ontological principle.

SUBJECTIVE AIM AND DECISION

For several centuries Western science has undertaken to exclude teleology, that is, any form of purpose, from nature. As nature has been extended, especially through evolutionary theory, to include human beings, there is a tendency to devalue or even deny purposiveness in human experience as well. Explanation should be exclusively in terms of efficient causation or the subsumption of particular events under general laws. This has proved an important corrective of the easy teleological explanations with which thinkers sometimes rested content in the Middle Ages.

Whitehead shared the common view of the great importance of efficient causes or what he called "**causal efficacy**." He was convinced that only actual entities exercise causal efficacy. They are the only "**reasons**." In other words, the content and form of any occasion is explained by actual entities. Any explanation that falls short of showing which actual entities have caused an occasion to have the form it has, has not completed its task. To say we have a heart in order to pump blood through the body fails to provide the reason for the existence and functioning of the heart.

Nevertheless, Whitehead believed that modern thought has gone too far in its rejection of teleology. For Whitehead, all experience is purposive.

Each occasion "**aims**" at achieving some **value.** Indeed it aims both at realizing some value in and of itself and also at contributing some value to future occasions. Every occasion has this "**subjective aim.**"

The aim of an occasion is not at **value** in general, but at some particular realization of value that is possible in that situation. In general, value is attained by generating and heightening "**contrasts.**" There are many diversities in the **past** that are most easily dealt with by elimination. But it is also possible in some instances to include diversities by incorporating them in a higher synthesis. The diverse features are thereby contrasted with one another. There are also contrasts between what is given in the past and relevant possibilities newly felt in **conceptual feelings**. The **reverted feelings** discussed above come into being in order to give greater **intensity** to the **satisfaction** and in that way to increase the value of the present realization. In a normal human experience we can find many contrasts and even contrasts of contrasts.

Needless to say, the aim of most occasions is completely unconscious. Even in conscious occasions, the aim is generally not consciously in view. Nevertheless, it influences the whole **process** of **concresecence.**

All occasions have some indeterminacy in their origins. Their **actual worlds** do not fully settle what they will become. Their **conceptual feelings** can include **reverted** ones that thus introduce alternatives. They can "**value up**" and "**value down**" parts of what they inherit. How they deal with what is indeterminate is affected by the aim.

However, the occasion completes itself as something entirely determinate. This involves cutting off all possibilities except one. This is its "**decision.**" This decision is its own. It is not determined by past occasions or by **God**. Accordingly, the **ontological principle** that every **reason** for what an occasion becomes is found in some actual entity does not deny that each occasion also includes an element of self-determination. Whitehead uses the Latin phrase "*causa sui*" to express this idea. Every occasion is in part causa sui. The decision of an occasion is its own act, and along with the decisions of all previous occasions and of God, it explains why the occasion is what it is.

COORDINATE AND GENETIC DIVISION OF ACTUAL OCCASIONS

It is of primary importance to recognize that actual occasions are in fact "atomic" in the original sense of that term. That is, it is not possible to divide an actual occasion into smaller entities. Therefore, the term "division," used here by Whitehead, is misleading. It would be less misleading to speak of the analysis of actual occasions.

Such analysis can be done in two ways. What Whitehead calls **"coordinate division"** is analysis into the **prehensions** of which it is constituted. These prehensions go through the process of **concrescence**. Each prehension, like the occasion as a whole, has its **datum** and its **subjective form.** The datum may be another actual occasion or **nexus**. It may be an **eternal object**. It may be some form of integration of these. In any case the prehension also has a **subjective form**. It is integrated into the **satisfaction** along with all the other prehensions.

When physicists are studying the transmission of energy through time, they may not be interested in the occasions as a whole but only in those prehensions that transmit the energy in question. Thus for some purposes the way the **prehension** is integrated into an actual occasion may not be important. The coordinate division yields the entities that are required.

The other form of analysis is called **"genetic division."** Much of the *Process and Reality* deals with this. It may be applied to individual **prehensions,** and this was done briefly in the discussion of prehensions in the preceding paragraphs. But the genetic division of the occasion as a whole includes more than that. It traces the stages from the initiation of a new occasion through to its completion in **satisfaction.** It treats the **phases** in the **process** of concrescence, and it will be spelled out in the next two sections.

CONCRESCENCE AND TIME

Concrescence is simply the process of becoming "concrete." Concrete means fully actual, and that means a completed actual occasion. The use of the term "concrescence" places emphasis on the idea that even these momentary flashes of actuality that Whitehead calls actual occasions are **processes**. There is the actual occasion in the process of becoming, and then there is the completed occasion. Whitehead calls the completion "**satisfaction.**" This term emphasizes that this process of becoming is characterized by **subjectivity.** There is a **subjective aim**, a **subjective form**, a **decision**, and a satisfaction. But as soon as the occasion attains satisfaction it becomes an **objective datum** for successor occasions.

Ordinarily, to think of a **process** is to think of earlier and later segments of the process. Whitehead uses that language at times. But he warns us against interpreting this language or the concrescence itself in a **temporal** way. In an important sense, it all happens at once. Viewed externally, the occasion is either there as **datum** to be prehended or it is not. It is never partially there. Furthermore, everything that happens in the process of concrescence presupposes the unity that is its outcome. If we think in temporal terms, this does not make sense. One might say, nevertheless, that the process is "temporal" but not in the sense of clock time that functions in physics or in ordinary language. It would be a unique sort of temporality, which Whitehead calls microscopic process. Hence, although Whitehead uses such temporal language as "earlier" and "later," he denies that the **phases** of concrescence are related temporally to one another. From the point of view of what he calls **time**, the occasion occurs all at once. Time derives from the succession of occasions.

"Earlier," in this context, can only mean prerequisite to "later." A **pure physical prehension** and a **pure conceptual prehension** must exist in order that they be synthesized. This does not mean that there is a *time* when the two prehensions exist separately and another *time* at which they are united in a **physical purpose**. They are found, so to speak, only in their unity. Nevertheless, the feelings as distinguishable from one another are presupposed by their synthesis.

To make some intuitive sense of this I suggest that one reflect on the experience of a driver who suddenly finds herself in danger and responds to it. This can happen in a "split second." She sees a car coming at her, she sees the location and movement of other cars, and she sees that there is just one way of braking and swerving that will avoid a collision. The situation and the reasoning that supports the **decision** are very complex. To explain why she acted as she did might take some time. But in fact the decision is almost instantaneous. The complex calculations involved include several *stages*. Some parts presuppose other parts. But they occur all at once. The point is that a complex **process**, analyzable into stages, can take place in a moment.

PHASES OF CONCRESCENCE

Even if a **concrescence** occurs, temporally speaking, all at once, to understand it requires analysis into the stages or **phases** of its becoming. Much of *Process and Reality* is an account of these phases. The concrescence can be analyzed **genetically** in more than one way, resulting in naming and counting the phases differently. Given the fact that these phases have no separate existence, we do not have correct and incorrect analyses. For different purposes we may analyze the concrescence somewhat differently. Whitehead calls this the **genetic analysis** of the occasion. We trace the outcome to its origins.

One simple analysis is into the **initial** or "**conformal**" phase, the "**supplementary**" phase, and the **satisfaction**. The conformal phase is that in which the new occasion reenacts the past. This is the **causal efficacy** of other actual entities for the present concrescing occasion. **Physical feelings**, both **pure** and **hybrid** take place in this phase. In most of the world this is the dominant factor. It establishes the endurance of things.

Nevertheless, no occasion is simply the reenactment of the **past.** One reason is that even if an occasion in an **enduring object** (that is, a **society** in which there is only one member at a time) derives much of its content from its immediate predecessor, it is also prehending other occasions. It takes account of its entire **actual world**, and that cannot be exactly the same as that of its predecessor. The new occasion must integrate what it receives from many sources, but it can do that only if it appropriates those sources selectively. This applies even to its predecessor in the enduring object. Thus even conformation to the past introduces a measure of novelty.

The **supplementary phase** begins with **conceptual feelings**. The **pure potentials** or **eternal objects** that characterize the data of the **physical feelings** are felt not only as they have **ingressed** into, or been actualized in, the past occasions but also as **pure potentials**. A **pure potential** may play the same role in the new occasion as in the old, but this is not inevitable. The new occasion may **intensify** or reduce the role of the feelings it feels in the past occasion in its reenactment of much of that occasion. This is the **valuing up** or **down** discussed above.

For example, suppose in one moment I am taking some satisfaction in the misfortune of a competitor. In the next moment that satisfaction may be qualified by sympathy. I am not condemned to retain the same **subjective form** of feeling indefinitely.

The importance of the derivation of **conceptual feelings** from **physical** ones is evident in ordinary sense perception. I see a patch of yellow. Only the most naïve realist supposes that what is objectively and independently present in the **region** where I see the yellow is very much like the yellow I see there. Nor is it very much like what is going on in my eye or in the occipital lobe of my brain. What is going on in the external region and in my eyes and in the occipital lobe are primarily physical **events**.

But what is given to me in **the mode of presentational immediacy** is an **eternal object**.

This example is taken from high grade experience, but Whitehead was impressed that the elementary entities that endure are typically **vibratory**. They appear to alternate between two states rather than simply repeat one of them. This is not a function of the slightly different **actual world**. Instead it involves a **conceptual feeling** derived, not from the actual world but from the ordering of **eternal objects**. These are **reverted feelings**.

I have focused on the simpler aspects of **supplementation: conceptual feelings** and **reverted feelings**. In subsequent sub-phases, under the broad heading of the **supplementary phase**, we can add **physical purposes** and, in more complex occasions, **propositional feelings**, and **intellectual feelings**.

All of this and more culminates in the **satisfaction** of the occasion. This is the completion of that occasion. It is also the beginning of its activity in informing successor occasions.

SUBJECTIVE IMMEDIACY AND CONSCIOUSNESS

The process of **concrescence** is the self-creation of the occasion. It is the **subject** or recipient of the **causal efficacy** of the past and it is the subject that integrates and transforms what it receives. It takes what is given to it objectively and constitutes itself as a new subject. In the moment of its **concrescence** it enjoys its own experience. That does not mean that it prehends that experience. Whitehead uses the term "**enjoy**" to emphasize that this is not a **datum** for something else, but the reality of the occasion itself, in itself, and for itself. The term suggests that to be in this way is something positive. It does not exclude pain or suffering. The point is that in the **concrescence** there is "**subjective immediacy.**"

We all know what s**ubjective immediacy** is. It is the way our experience feels to us at all times. But when we think of it, we almost necessarily have **conscious** subjective immediacy in mind. To understand Whitehead, we must grasp that there is also nonconscious subjective immediacy, indeed, that the vast majority of subjective immediacy is not conscious.

We can begin by recognizing that much of the time we are not conscious of our own **emotions**. Others may see that we are embarrassed or angry, and we may deny it. Sometimes, of course, the denial may be a lie, but at other times it expresses ignorance. Psychologists may train us to pay attention to our emotions. The point is simply that the emotions are there in subjective immediacy whether we are aware of them or not.

In this example, we are dealing with **emotions** that are part of a conscious experience although not themselves conscious. Also we are dealing with emotions to which consciousness can be directed. But we should notice that becoming conscious of these emotions, at least in Whitehead's view, is becoming conscious here and now of the emotion of the preceding occasion. No occasion can be conscious of itself. It cannot prehend itself at all. It is largely constituted by its **prehension** of other occasions. The subjective immediacy of an occasion may include consciousness, but this is never consciousness of itself. It in no way assumes consciousness or depends upon it.

Consciousness depends on the "**affirmation/negation contrast**". To be conscious that something exists implicitly involves the awareness that it might not exist. To be conscious of my own feelings is to be aware of the possibility of different feelings. In **the phases of concrescence,** this contrast comes into play with **intellectual feelings**, the contrast of the **proposition** with the occasion or nexus from which its **logical subject** is derived. These are of central importance for human experience and in general for that of other animals with nervous systems. Whether they occur elsewhere is problematic. In any case, the vast majority of occasions complete themselves with **physical purposes**. Their feelings are subjectively immediate, but they are not conscious.

In the evolutionary process, therefore, the most likely scenario is that when central nervous systems developed to a certain point, the **final percipient occasion** became conscious of some elements of its experience. In such occasions, in addition to continuing nonconscious **physical purposes**, some stimuli gave rise to **propositional** and **intellectual feelings**. These involved the **affirmation/negation** contrast and included consciousness in their **subjective forms.** Of course, most of the experience of occasions that included conscious feelings remained nonconscious.

I have used **"consciousness"** as a convenient way to talk about the quality or character of what emerged with the development of central nervous systems. In Whitehead it is important that the term is not used to identify anything that is actual in itself. It points to one of the **subjective forms** of some of the **prehensions** of some actual occasions. It is not a name for experience like that of human beings. We should not juxtapose consciousness to physical reality as often happens when physical reality is supposed to be constituted of **"matter."** The prehensions whose subjective forms include consciousness, that is, conscious feelings, are constituted in part by **physical feelings**.

OBJECTIVE IMMORTALITY

The state of an occasion that is the alternative to **subjective immediacy** is **objective immortality.** In its attainment of **satisfaction**, the occasion becomes a **datum** for other occasions. It immediately begins to play a role in their subjective self-constitution. In that **process** it does not change. It remains forever what it has become even though it plays different roles in different successors and is interpreted differently by them. In itself, as objectively given for other occasions, it is "immortal."

Sometimes, the notion of "objective" is misunderstood. We get our sense of "objects" from what is given to us in **presentational immediacy**. To be an object is supposed to be something like a stone or a building. But the actual occasions that have become objects are moments of experience. Their primary characteristic is **emotion.** What are **objectively immortal** are better thought of as past bursts of emotion. When they are felt or prehended in their objective immortality, there is some conformation on the part of the new occasion to their emotion. The difference between **subjective immediacy** and objective immortality is largely that between present emotion and past emotion. It is between having emotion and transmitting emotion to another.

This is, of course, oversimplified. For Whitehead the **subjective form** of an occasion is not exhausted by **emotion.** But most of the other elements mentioned by Whitehead—**valuations, purposes, aversions** and **adversions**—are closely related to emotion. The one exception is consciousness. Also, the emotion of one occasion is always the subjective form of **prehensions** of other occasions and **eternal objects**, and it is felt as such in the new occasion. If we abstract emotions from the **data** of the feelings whose **subjective forms** they are, we misunderstand them. Nevertheless, this oversimplification should guide understanding better than the usual view of the nature of objects. What is objectively immortal is feeling.

The word "immortal" can also mislead. In the classical world it was virtually synonymous with divinity. In Whitehead it has no such connotation. His point is that whatever occurs is forever a part of the **past** out of which new occasions arise. It no longer **enjoys subjective immediacy**. In that sense, as a **subject,** it has **perished**. But in this **perished**, objective state, it remains unchangingly whatever it was when it occurred.

MICROSCOPIC AND MACROSCOPIC PROCESS

"Process" is a comprehensive term for all that is going on. It is not inclusive of the whole of reality. In addition to the process, there is also potentiality of various types, especially the **pure potentials** or **eternal objects**. This book is entitled *Process and Reality*. But everything actual is in process. Apart from the actual, there is no **potential**. The **eternal objects** would not even be "real."

It is not hard to understand that there is a great difference between the **concrescence** of the many into the one momentary occasion and the vast flow of **events** that is our habitual experience. Once we have accepted the idea that there are distinct occasions of experience we are brought to this distinction. Clearly their becoming is different from the becoming of a tree or a human person. What remains is to clarify this distinction.

In Whitehead's terminology, not all process is **temporal**. **Time** depends on the **macroscopic process,** which involves the "**transition**" from one occasion, functioning as a cause to its successors, which are affected by it. The **microscopic process** of **concrescence** is not **temporal**. This broad distinction is clear.

There is perplexity, however, in understanding in detail the relation of the microscopic and the macroscopic, of **concrescence** and **transition**. The problem is that our habit of mind, formed in relation to the macroscopic process, wants a clear **temporal** sequence, with concrescence completed before transition begins. We want to say that first concrescence achieves **satisfaction**. Only at that point in "**time**" does a new concrescence begin. However, Whitehead pictures the **satisfaction** of one occasion as functioning **causally** in the constitution of its successors. Thus the satisfaction of one occasion is already the initiation of a new concrescence.

Nevertheless, Whitehead distinguishes the **process** of "the many becoming one" from that in which the new one functions as part of the many that are becoming another one. The many becoming one is guided by an **aim** to attain a particular definiteness. This microscopic process is teleological. The **transition** from being the goal of a process to being a requirement laid on a future process, from teleology to efficient causality, is the macroscopic process. Of course, each mode of process presupposes the other. They are not separable.

CREATIVITY AS THE ULTIMATE

"**Concrescence**" focuses attention on the inner dynamics of the becoming of a single occasion. It presupposes that there have been other occasions and that there will be new ones in the future. "**Creativity**" directs attention equally to concrescence and **transition**. At every instant the many, the vast many, are becoming one in a myriad of occasions. The becoming of each of these occasions adds a new one to that myriad. Whereas "concrescence" focuses on the individual subjective act of becoming, "creativity" draws attention to the ever ongoing **process** through which the cosmos continues in being. It is the way of denoting the ultimate fact that "the many become one and are increased by one."

Whitehead identifies **creativity** as "the **ultimate**." It is that of which every actual entity is an instance. It plays the role in Whitehead that "being itself" plays in the Thomistic tradition. In that tradition to be is to be an instance of being. In Whitehead to be actual is to be an instance of creativity. In Thomism being itself is beyond all attributes or characteristics. In Whitehead, likewise, creativity has no character of its own, in the sense that it is open equally to any and all **eternal objects** and is in itself characterized by none.

Using different labels for what is ultimate does not in itself determine that there are metaphysical differences. Thomas identified "being itself" as the "act of being." One could regard Whitehead's work as explaining what an act of being is, i.e., the unification of the many. Thomism may not be closed to that possibility. However, the term "being itself" easily suggests something more static and substantial, that is, something *underlying* all diversity and particularity. In some formulations it seems that being itself might even exist without embodiment in particular instantiations. "The many becoming one" cannot underlie anything and certainly cannot exist or occur except in particular instances.

It may be that the discussion of what is ultimate has played a lager role in India than in the West. Brahman is the traditional Hindu ultimate and is very much like being itself. Buddhists found the understanding of Brahman to be substantialist, and they rejected it. In one important form of Buddhism, they affirmed instead that everything is an instance of *pratitya samutpada* or dependent origination. The similarity to Whitehead's creativity is striking.

Whitehead's own comparisons are with the "neutral stuff" affirmed by some of his contemporaries and with the 'prime matter" of the Aristotelian tradition. In other words, by the "ultimate" he means that of which all things consist. It is the ultimate "material cause" in Aristotle's sense. But for Whitehead the "material cause" is definitely not **matter.** Metaphysically, and in physics as well, "matter" is fundamentally passive. For Whitehead, creativity could be thought of as activity itself. It is closer to what physicists mean by energy than what is connoted when they speak of matter.

In any case, one cannot go beyond creativity to its material **cause** or to any other cause. One can describe how it expresses itself, but one cannot meaningfully ask why creativity, and not something else, is the way the world is. There is no "**reason**" for creativity.

Sometimes the reader of Whitehead is likely to project into "creativity" more than he intends. He does cause us to marvel that whatever happens, the **process** of bringing new occasions out of old ones continues. Creation is fundamental and ongoing. There is always something new. But what is new may not be better than what is old. Occasions that occur in the **process** of the decay and dying of larger organisms, such as human beings, are also instances of creativity, no more and no less than those that bring new life into being. Creativity is completely neutral from a moral perspective. Mutual slaughter consists in instances of creativity just as does the composition of a symphony. Also one cannot speak of more and less creativity. Like ultimates in other traditions, creativity is beyond good and evil or any quantification.

GOD

Whitehead is unusual among twentieth-century thinkers in seeing a large role for **God** in the explanation of what happens in the world. This understanding came late in his philosophical development. "God" first appeared in additions to the Lowell Lectures of 1925 included in the published version of *Science and the Modern World.*

Whitehead found that neither **creativity** nor individual occasions could explain the role **eternal objects** play in constituting a new occasion. The new occasion does not simply reenact the eternal objects derived from its **actual world**. We saw that the **supplementary phase** of a **concrescence** is more complex than that. It assumes a particular order among the eternal objects that is not explained by what the eternal objects are in themselves.

For example, there is **reversion**. Even though each photonic occasion reverts to the character of the one before the last, this requires that there be an order of the **eternal objects**. This is even more true when more complex matters are considered. Without an order among eternal objects the regularities that are thought of as natural laws would not obtain. Both novelty and regularity presuppose such an order. The order among eternal objects makes possible the increase of **value** in the world.

According to the **ontological principle,** the **eternal objects** as such are not the **reasons** for their own roles in the world. That reason must be found in an actual entity. This actual entity must be cosmic in its functioning. Whitehead calls it **God.** God is the one actual entity that is not an actual occasion.

In an earlier section we considered the fact that actual occasions are purposive. They **aim** to attain some **value** in themselves and through their influence on others. This purposive character of actual occasions cannot be explained by **creativity** as such or by an **occasion's actual world. Eternal objects** are ordered by God with a view to eliciting greater value in the world. Actual occasions **prehend pure potentials** for their realization as ordered in this way. Thus they derive from God an "**initial aim**" at realizing what is possible in that situation.

God's ordering of **eternal objects** thus functions as the basis of regularity in the world, the basis of novelty, and the basis of purposiveness. Whitehead believes that this ordering is the work of an actual entity. This actual entity evokes worship from human beings, and this justifies naming it "God." However, Whitehead is emphatic that some of the characteristics attributed to God in some theistic traditions are not justified by this account. For example, God is not the "**ultimate**." God is an instance of **creativity**. God does not control what happens. There are many "**reasons**" for what happens in every event, of which God is always only one; that is God never unilaterally determines what happens. Still God is always one of these reasons, the one who calls for the realization of optimum **value** and makes that realization possible.

We noted above that **creativity** is the **ultimate**. God does not appear in Whitehead's categoreal scheme. He declares "God" to be a "derivative notion." Also, he describes God as a "creature" or even an "accident" of **creativity**. This seems to differentiate what he calls "God" radically from what has usually been understood as "God" in the Abrahamic traditions.

There are real differences between the dominant Western understanding of God and that of Whitehead, but these differences should not be overstated. Although Whitehead does not describe God as "**ultimate**," attributing that status to **creativity,** he does assert that God primordially provides a "character" to creativity. Without that character no actual occasion can come into being, and, of course, apart from actual occasions, there is no creativity. Accordingly, God is as metaphysically necessary for creativity as creativity is metaphysically necessary for God. The importance of the apparently belittling language is to emphasize that God is not the unilateral cause of any actual occasion, much less of the world as a whole. In *Science and the Modern World,* Whitehead emphasizes that if God were the *ultimate*, God would be as responsible for the terrible evils in the world as for the good. For Whitehead such a God would not evoke worship.

Whitehead sees in the theory of Plato and the life of Jesus the ideal of persuasive power in distinction from controlling or coercive power. He judges that most views of divine power, including those of most people in the Abrahamic tradition, are projections on the cosmos of the characteristics of human emperors. He thinks that finding God revealed in this kind of controlling power has done enormous damage in human history. He avoids any language about God that would associate his view of God with this widespread form of theism.

THE PRIMORDIAL AND CONSEQUENT NATURES OF GOD

Whitehead calls God's ordering of **eternal objects** for the sake of realizing **value** in the world, God's **"primordial nature."** He thinks of this ordering as a single nontemporal act, preceding and conditioning every actual occasion. The meaning of "primordial" here is much the same as the more usual term "eternal." Hence one may say that God is eternal. God has no beginning and no end.

However, Whitehead speculates that God's primordial nature does not exhaust what God is. According to the **ontological principle**, in order that God be the **reason** for anything in the world, God must be an actual entity. The primordial nature of God can be thought of as the **conceptual pole** of God. But for actual occasions, the conceptual pole by itself is not actual. What is actual is the **dipolar occasion**, physical as well as conceptual. Unless God is actual, God cannot be the **reason** for the order of **potentials** that, in turn, provides order and novelty to the world. But for God to be actual would seem to require that God have **physical feelings** as well as **conceptual** ones. Those physical feelings would be and, Whitehead speculates, are, God's prehensions of actual occasions. These prehensions constitute God's **physical pole** and complete God. This aspect of God is affected by everything that happens in the world. It is in this sense "consequent" upon the world. Whitehead calls the physical pole of God, the **"consequent nature."**

Although Whitehead proposes that all actual entities, including God, have basic similarities such as **dipolarity**, he speculates that God differs markedly from actual occasions. These originate in conformation to the **actual world** and God. Thus their first phase is their **physical pole**. This is taken up in the **supplementary phase** and integrated with **conceptual feelings**. Thus the occasion comes to **satisfaction** only through its **conceptual pole**. God, on the other hand, originates in the **conceptual feelings** that constitute the **mental pole** or **primordial nature**. This is forever unchanged. God's **physical feelings** are woven upon it, thus constituting the **"consequent nature."** This consequent nature cannot be separated from the primordial nature. Indeed, what God is at any moment, is consequent upon events in the world, that is, the consequent nature of God, always includes the primordial nature. In actual occasions it is the addition of conceptual feelings to physical feelings and the **contrasts** that addition makes possible that give rise to consciousness. In God, it is the addition of physical feelings to the conceptual ones that introduces consciousness.

Another difference is that actual occasions exist as subjects only momentarily and then pass into **objective immortality**. In **living persons,** the **subjective feelings** of one occasion are reenacted in its successors with a certain **immediacy**, but this quickly fades. **God** is everlasting. The consequent nature retains all that enters it in full immediacy. Thus the value that is attained and quickly lost in the world is everlasting in God. It is the immediacy of feeling in the actual occasions that is objectively immortal in God.

Most references to **God** in Whitehead's writings are to the **primordial nature.** This plays a metaphysically central role. Whitehead considers his account of the **consequent nature** as a plausible and reasonable one, adding to the coherence of his philosophy. In explaining it here, I have emphasized, as has Whitehead, the **speculative** nature of these theories. Since Whitehead describes his entire conceptual scheme as speculative, this description does not in itself distinguish the concept of the status of the account of the consequent nature of God from that of other concepts. However, Whitehead thinks that many of his theories can be tested in experience and that, in general, they pass the test. Testing of the idea that God has a consequent nature is harder and less reliable, although Whitehead thinks there are religious **intuitions** and features of religious experience that support the idea.

The more limited grounding of this doctrine does not mean that for Whitehead the consequent nature is readily dispensable. There is strong pragmatic support. For Whitehead the belief that the ephemeral values of the world are preserved in God is required, if life is to be found meaningful.

PERPETUAL PERISHING

The existential or religious importance for Whitehead of the **consequent mature** of God results from his vision of actual occasions as **"perpetually perishing."** This idea needs fuller clarification. It appears to be in some tension with the notion of **objective immortality** and also of the idea that in a **living person** past occasions are summed up in the present one.

Accordingly, before focusing on perpetual perishing, we should consider further Whitehead's view of the status of the **past.** We should begin by recognizing that Whitehead views the past as "actual." He speaks of the "**actual world**" and "**past actual** occasions." Since "actual" implies acting, some of his interpreters have thought that this was careless on Whitehead's part. They have argued that prehending and deciding are the only forms of acting, and that, accordingly, only **concrescing** occasions act. What is past, they think, cannot be actual.

However, Whitehead does not agree. A **concrescence** is an instance of the many becoming one, and in that **process** the many are acting just as much as the one. Whatever has happened plays some role in the becoming of the new occasion. For it to do so is for it to be actual.

Some ask how this can be. They want to know "where" the past now is. The "where" has, for such questioners, a predominantly spatial connotation. And the "now" implies that the space would have to be in the present. But for Whitehead, the "where" should be understood four dimensionally, and the answer is that past occasions are in the past portion of the **extensive continuum**, just where they occurred. This means that Whitehead is a full-fledged realist with respect to the past. The past has not perished in the sense of having totally ceased to exist. On the contrary, it has become **objectively immortal**.

What then is perpetually perishing? The answer is that the "**subjective immediacy**" of an actual occasion no sooner happens than it ceases to be. Yet even this should be qualified. In a **living person**, the very recent past still has its own **immediacy** in the present. The antecedent parts of a musical phrase are still functioning with their **subjective forms** as one hears the new note and integrates the subjective form of hearing it with the earlier ones. The **immediacy** has not perished, although its **subject** has. Nevertheless the immediacy fades, and it, too, soon perishes.

The intrinsic **value**, the **intensity** of feeling, of an occasion lies in its **subjective form**. Even if some of this, in the special case of **living persons**, continues on a little while, it is gone soon enough. The perishing of what is of **value** seems to have the last word. For Whitehead, and for many others as well, this disappearance of all that seems worth achieving undercuts the worthwhileness of the achievement. Perpetual perishing is the **ultimate** evil, not it the sense of being the worst, but in the sense of being part of the ultimate nature of things.

The response to this evil is in **God's** retention of the **values** achieved in actual occasions. That is, God retains the **immediacy** of each occasion. This is like the partial retention of immediacy by one occasion of human experience of its predecessor. In that case, there is a different **subject,** that is, a new occasion, quickly succeeded by another and then another. The immediacy of **enjoyment** in the earlier occasion continues in the new ones, but it is quickly diluted in the transition from one to another with all the new stimuli. God similarly retains the immediacy of enjoyment of the occasion. But the actual entity, God, is everlasting. The reasons that immediacy fades so quickly in human experience do not apply. We can believe that in God the immediacy does not perish. The value of all that has been forever enriches the divine life. The values achieved in creaturely existence endure.

Initial Aim

Whitehead affirms that purposiveness characterizes the subjective existence of all occasions. They all **aim** at a creative synthesis of the **prehensions** that arise from their physical **data.** This aim does not arise from the actual occasions that constitute its **actual world**, although it is directed at the particular value that is possible given the actual world of the occasion.

It arises from the ordering of **pure potentiality** by the divine aim at the realization of **intensity**. The occasion prehends certain possibilities as they are felt in **God's primordial nature**, that is, with the aim at their realization. This realization can occur only as a particular integration of the prehensions of the occasion's actual world.

The initial aim is more exactly described as the initial **phase** of the **subjective aim**. The **subjective aim** is affected not only by its initial derivation from the **primordial nature** of **God** but also by the occasion's whole inheritance from its **actual world**. What the aim will be in the **satisfaction** of the occasion is not settled by its origins in God.

We may assume that in the vast majority of the occasions that make up the world the final form of the **subjective aim** will not differ in any significant way from its initial form. In human experience, however, especially among theists, the sense of the difference is quite important. In *Religion in the Making* Whitehead writes of a "rightness in things partly realized and partly missed," believing that a sense of such a gap or tension is widely felt in many human societies. One feels called to be open to criticism, but actually responds defensively. One feels called to forgive a minor injury but continues to resent. That is, among the impulses operative in any moment of human experience, the theist is likely to understand some as derived from **God** and others as arising in one's social context, in one's past, and in one's body. Whitehead's analysis undergirds this way of thinking. Of course, it is not easy to know what is really derived from God.

Interpreters disagree on some points. Is the initial aim always at a very specific **satisfaction** or is it a more general lure toward realization of **value?** Does it include the whole **lure of God** in the occasion, or is it to be distinguished from the lure to particular **conceptual reversions?** What can be said with confidence is that God is the **reason** that more than one outcome is possible from the physical **data** and that God's aim is the realization of the greatest value possible.

INTENSITY

I have spoken generally of what **God aims** to increase in the world as **"value."** This is one of many cases where a common word is both necessary to point to what is to be discussed and inadequate. In many philosophies value is a function of human valuing; so the focus is on what people want or *should* want. In economics the value of anything is the price it brings in the market place. As long as the world is thought of as composed of physical objects in motion, this focus on human desires is virtually inevitable.

For Whitehead, on the other hand, human valuing is by no means central. The world is made up of present and past subjects. To be a **subject** is to be something for itself. There are better and worse ways of being something for itself. Thus the question of human desire is irrelevant to the basic question of the **value** of things in themselves. Each actual occasion was what it was with the value that it had. One can also speak of the value that it contributes to later occasions, and this is also quite independent of human desire.

The values of occasions vary in many ways. One of these differences can be described in terms of more or less. But what characteristic of one occasion makes it more valuable than another? In *Process and Reality* Whitehead uses the term **"intensity."** The feelings of one occasion have greater intensity than the feelings of another and also contribute more to the intensity of feeling in successor occasions. **God** primordially orders **pure potentials** in such a way as to evoke increased intensity of feeling in the world. The evolutionary advance to central nervous systems is an *advance* because central nervous systems make possible far more intense experiences than are possible without them.

Whitehead devotes considerable attention to what occurs in the process of **concrescence** that increases intensity. The simplest answer is that this is accomplished by **contrast**, and that beyond simple contrasts there are contrasts of contrasts, and contrasts of contrasts of contrasts. But Whitehead also provides more detailed analysis. He shows that the most intense experiences require **"harmony"** arising from the right combination of **"width"** and **"narrowness."** Width points to the need for variety in the **data** of the occasion. Within this width, concentration and focus are needed, and this is made possible by narrowness. This narrowness is achieved by the **social ordering** of much of the environment. **Transmutation** makes it possible to ignore the great variety of occasions within a **society** and objectify it as a single entity. This entails **"vagueness"** in the prehension of the many occasions that make up the society.

Those **nexūs** that are not social constitute **"chaos."** Because their contributions tend to cancel each other out rather than make **contrasts** possible, their contribution to the occasion is **"triviality."** The intensity of experience requires triviality and **vagueness** to support **width** and **narrowness**.

The main point is that various kinds of simplification are necessary to the becoming of any intense experience. **Transmutation** simplifies the experience of the **societies** that constitute so important a part of the environment. This gives the needed order. But for novelty to flourish, there must also be parts of the environment that are not ordered in this way. **Chaos** also makes its contribution.

It may be well to note that in later writings Whitehead continues to search for a term that provides a measure of **value.** Part Four of *Adventures of Ideas* is his most elaborate contribution to value theory. There "**strength of beauty**" corresponds closely to what is meant in *Process and Reality* by "**intensity,**" but it does not exhaust what is valuable. In *Modes of Thought,* Whitehead proposes "importance."

Strain Feelings

That there is **perception in the mode of presentational immediacy** is indisputable. It dominates **consciousness** and provides us with the clearest part of our experience. It can be denied primacy in experience, but it must be explained.

Most of the time Whitehead writes as though all feelings are either **physical** or **conceptual** or some combination of these. But "**strain feelings**" do not fit this classification. **Physical feelings** relate us to what has just happened, the immediate **past,** and through that to the more remote past. But in **presentational immediacy** we are not looking back into the past. Conceptual feelings are certainly involved, but as we have discussed them so far, they are related to what is **felt physically**, which is past. In vision, the most vivid case of perception in the mode of presentational immediacy, the **eternal objects,** are located at relatively remote points in space, not in the **region** of the brain from which they were most immediately derived. The spatio-temporal region where presentational immediacy locates them is not identical with the spatio-temporal region where, in normal vision, the physical stimulus arose. Some other kind of feeling is involved. Whitehead recognized this, and he introduced what he called "**strain feelings.**" These are feelings of the locus on which eternal objects are projected in presentational immediacy.

Strain feelings orient us spatially. Kant had argued that space and time as well as causality are involuntary creations of the human mind. Whitehead as a realist believes that relations among actual occasions construct a four dimensional space-time **continuum**. This is given for us.

As a geometrician he can also define **straight lines**. As a metaphysician he has to show that the actual occasion of human experience can project straight lines in all directions and thereby gain needed knowledge about how to operate. Presumably other animals do this as well. These straight lines define the present for an occasion within its inertial system.

Once strain feelings are established, the projection of **eternal objects** in line with these feelings can be, at least in a general way, understood. Since there is little doubt that something of this sort happens, we have no choice but to believe this added wonder of human experience. Whitehead grounds the production of strain feelings in bodily experience.

The most obvious role of strain feelings is as the basis of the **presentational immediacy** that dominates our conscious experience. However, they have additional functions. All the strains defined by the strain feelings of an occasion together provide the "**strain locus**" of the occasion. We might think of this as the space in which the occasion locates itself. This is the basis not only of the subjective experience of rest and motion but also of their physical effects. Individual actual occasions do not move, but **enduring objects** do. This motion is a physical fact for the occasions making up the enduring object. It depends on strain feelings defining the space or strain locus in which they exist. In relation to that space an enduring object may be at rest or in motion. Motion is relative when we are speaking of diverse inertial systems, but within an inertial system it is a physical fact.

Strains provide the meaning of straightness The experience of straightness is presupposed by measurement and so cannot be defined by it. This is fundamental for science and mathematics. The definition of a straight line as the shortest distance between two points presupposes measurement, which presupposes straightness. Whitehead provides ways of defining basic geometric terms that do not presuppose measurement.

THE EXTENSIVE CONTINUUM AND ITS REGIONS

The "**extensive continuum**" is Whitehead's name for what most physicists call "**space-time.**" Whitehead's reason for using a different technical term is that when we say space-time we bring with us the connotations that those terms have borne for centuries, whereas he thinks that we need a more fundamental re-thinking. Space-time could be understood as having an existence independent of occasions in which, then, occasions come into being. Whitehead rejects that idea. Einstein's space-time has physical properties such as curvature. Whitehead's extensive continuum as potential rather than actual is too abstract to have such properties. His thinking about this is informed by his work on geometry, and is not easy for those not versed in the mathematics fully to appreciate. In Part Four of *Process and Reality* Whitehead develops definitions of the geometrical elements from the characteristics of **extensive connection**. Extensive relations pervade our experience.

Actual occasions can be analyzed **coordinately** into their **prehensions** or **genetically** into the **phases of concrescence**. But they cannot be physically divided into these or any other parts. This means that what is actual is not a continuum. It is composed of actual occasions each of which has definite extension.

Nevertheless, these are "**extensively connected.**" These extensive connections are not actualities, but they are potentialities realized by the actual occasions. These potentialities are not atomic in the way the actual occasions that realize them are. On the contrary they constitute a continuum. This is the extensive continuum. The existence of the extensive continuum depends on the existence of the actual occasions, but given their actuality, the extensive continuum constitutes a restriction on all future occasions as well. They must exist in **extensive connection** to the present and past occasions and to one another.

The world we know is four-dimensional. However, this form of dimensionality is a contingent feature. Perhaps dimensionality as such is contingent. What is necessary to the **extensive continuum** is only that all occasions be extensively related.

This necessity of extensive relations implies also that the continuum can be analyzed into **regions** each of which has the characteristic of extensiveness and extensive relatedness to all other regions. Since we are dealing with a continuum no one division is more appropriate than any other. However, in point of fact, the actual occasions actualize the continuum in particular ways. Each has its "**standpoint**" within it. Many characteristics of an actual occasion depend upon its **regional standpoint**. For example, this standpoint determines just which occasions it prehends. The extensive continuum as such is not affected by the presence or absence of actual occasions.

Past, present, and future are not characteristics of the extensive continuum as such. They are defined in terms of prehensive relationships. The "**past**" of any occasion is everything that has **causal efficacy** for it. The "**future**" is constituted by those occasions that will be **causally** affected by it. The "**contemporary**" world is made up of all the occasions that are neither causally effective in the **occasion** in question nor causally affected by it. That is, **contemporaries** are occasions that do not affect one another. Thus temporal characteristics belong to actual occasions as a result of their prehensions and are not an independent feature of the extensive continuum.

Geometry is the study of regions. The relation of these regions to those actualized by occasions does not enter into geometry. But whatever is learned about such regions by geometry applies to the **regional standpoints** of actual occasions and, therefore, to the occasions themselves. In Part Four of *Process and Reality,* Whitehead develops the principles of geometry out of his study of the relation of regions. His definitions of terms are very exact. At only a few points does his mathematical work in Part Four impinge on the remainder of the book. It would serve no useful purpose to repeat his definitions in this glossary.

The indifference of the extensive continuum to which regions within it become the **standpoints** of actual occasions, points to an additional role of the **initial aim**. In every moment the **past** leaves open the exact way in which new occasions will actualize the extensive continuum. Exactly which regions will be the standpoints of actual occasions is indeterminate. Yet such determination cannot be left to the **decision** of the new occasions. The standpoint determines exactly what is included in the **actual world** of the occasion. Neither the actual world nor the new occasion can determine that. Whitehead proposes that this is determined by the primordial ordering of **pure potentials,** that is, the primordial nature of **God** through the initial aim of each occasion.

DURATIONS

In the dominant worldviews of the **past,** it has been assumed that there is a unique meaning to "the present" that applies equally throughout the universe. Relativity theory undercuts that idea. Nevertheless, the present from the perspective of any inertial system has a definite meaning. It will always consist in a **duration.**

A duration is a set of contiguous occasions stretching across the universe all of which are contemporaries of all the others. That is, no occasion in the duration is **causally** related to any other. Since the presence or absence of a particular **causal** relation is a physical characteristic of occasions, what is a duration from any point of view is a duration from all points of view. There is nothing relativistic about durations as such.

Any actual occasion is a member of many durations. To understand this, think of your relation to a star. Events in that star long ago influence you now because the light they emitted has reached the Earth. But many later events have occurred on that star that have not affected you in any way thus far. Each of those is a member of one of the durations of which your present experience is also a member. But most of them are not members of the same duration as most of the others. Most are organized temporally as earlier and later. Thus your experience in this moment, like any occasion, is a member of many different durations.

Relativity comes into play when we ask which of those durations constitutes the present. For us, this is the "presented duration," corresponding to our **strain locus.** We have a vivid sense that some of those **contemporary** events took place in the past and that there will be many future events that we will not affect. This is quite true in terms of our presented duration. But it is wrong to assume that this duration is objectively, and for every observer, the present. The evidence is now quite clear that this is not the case. What defines our sense of the present is the strain locus or inertial system within which we find ourselves. Other durations constitute the present for observers in other inertial systems. Whitehead built not only his special relativity theory but also his general relativity theory around multiple time systems.

I have written of the **strain locus** as well as the presented duration. They correspond closely, but they are not identical. The strain locus is a **region** of the **extensive continuum.** A presented duration constitutes a set of actual occasions.

Index

C

Canalized 43
Categories of existence **16**, 23, 27
Causal efficacy 19, 22, 31, 32, 35, 43, 52, 54, 55, 57, 61, 62, 77
Causality 20, 21, 33, 41, 57, 65, 67, 69, 78
Causa sui 58
Chaos 74, 75
Conceptual pole (mental) **40-41**, 69, 70
Concrescence 58, **59-60**, 61, 62, 63, 65, 66, 67, 71, 74, 77
  initial (conformal) phase 61
  phases 59, **60-62,** 63, 77
  supplementary phase 61, 62, 67, 70
Consciousness 20, 21, 34, 52, 53, **62-64,** 70, 75
Contemporary 78, 79
Contrast 46, 51, 52, 53, 58, 63, 70, 74
  affirmation/negation 51, 52, 53, 63
  generic **51-53**
Coordinate division of actual occasion **58-59**
Creativity 25, **66-67**, 68, 69

D

Data 18, 28, 32, 33, 35, 36, 37, 39, 40, 41, 42, 43, 52, 54, 56, 61, 64, 72, 73, 74
Datum 28, 31, 34, 37, 39, 40, 46, 47, 56, 59, 60, 62, 64
Decision **57-58,** 59, 60, 78
Dipolarity 41, 69, 70
Disbelief 52
Durations **78-79**

E

Emotion 26, 34, 35, 38, 39, 40, 41, 62, 63, 64
Empty space 19, 27, **28-29,** 30, 42
Enduring object **29-30,** 44, 61, 76
Enjoyment 62, 72

V

W